Foul Deeds & Suspicious Deaths In & Around Bradford

FOUL DEEDS AND SUSPICIOUS DEATHS Series

Wharncliffe's *Foul Deeds and Suspicious Deaths* series explores, in detail, crimes of passion, brutal murders and foul misdemeanours from early modern times to the present day. Victorian street crime, mysterious deaths and modern murders tell tales where passion, jealousy and social deprivation brought unexpected violence to those involved. From unexplained death and suicide to murder and manslaughter, the books provide a fascinating insight into the lives of both victims and perpetrators as well as society as a whole.

Other titles in the series include:

Please contact us via any of the methods below for more information or a catalogue.
WHARNCLIFFE BOOKS
47 Church Street – Barnsley – South Yorkshire S70 2AS
Tel: 01226 734555 – 734222; Fax: 01226 724438
E-mail: enquiries@pen-and-sword.co.uk
Website: www.wharncliffebooks.co.uk

Foul Deeds & Suspicious Deaths In & Around

BRADFORD

STEPHEN WADE

Series Editor
Brian Elliott

Wharncliffe Books

First Published in Great Britain in 2005 by
Wharncliffe Books
an imprint of
Pen and Sword Books Ltd
47 Church Street
Barnsley
South Yorkshire
S70 2AS

Copyright © Stephen Wade 2005

ISBN: 1-903425-83-2

Typeset in 11/13pt Plantin by Concept, Huddersfield.

Printed and bound in England by
CPI UK.

Pen and Sword Books Ltd incorporates the Imprints of
Pen & Sword Aviation, Pen & Sword Maritime,
Pen & Sword Military, Wharncliffe Books,
Pen & Sword Select, Pen and Sword Military Classics
and Leo Cooper.

For a complete list of Pen & Sword titles please contact
PEN & SWORD BOOKS LIMITED
47 Church Street
Barnsley
South Yorkshire
S70 2BR
England
E-mail: enquiries@pen-and-sword.co.uk
Website: www.pen-and-sword.co.uk

Contents

Introduction

The city of Bradford was one of the new cities of the Industrial Revolution. At the beginning of the nine-teenth century, its population was around 13,000; by 1901 the figure was almost 280,000. The geographic and economic facts are basic but extremely significant: in the heartland of the West Riding, central to the cloth trade, with its woollen and worsted industries, it was a place where, as J B Priestley reminded us in one of his many writings on Bradford, 'All the processes of worsted manufacture – combing, weaving, spinning, dyeing and finishing – are carried on.'

In Asa Briggs' magisterial study of Victorian cities, we are reminded that there have always been comparisons made between the city and its neighbour, Leeds: he calls Bradford 'a smaller and rougher town' and goes on, 'it was in some ways more of a world centre: "Worstedopolis" was the name given to it by both boasters and critics ...' Much can be made of that word 'rougher' but for present purposes, the focus is on some of the less healthy and unpleasant spin-offs of this rapid growth and concentration of industry. Priestley considered his native city to be 'entirely without charm, though not altogether ugly' but added that 'it has the good fortune to be on the edge of some of the most enchanting country in all England.' We need to be reminded, then, that some of the stories here took place in the idyllic tourist spot of Haworth.

Yet, it is not difficult to find trouble and lawlessness in the city well before the population expanded so markedly. A Victorian historian, W Cunningham, noted that in the year 1663 'a few persons from Bradford were implicated in the foolish Farnley Plot, the promoters of which wanted to over-throw monarchical government.' These rebels were executed at York. But of course, the Civil War came to the area as well: in 1642, the Earl of Newcastle brought a force of 9,000 men to take Bradford away from the citizens. This led a little later to the battle of Adwalton Moor at which Fairfax's Roundheads were beaten, and hence the famous story of Newcastle at Bolling Hall, where supposedly a ghost told him to 'Pity poor Bradford' and indeed he did so.

For reasons of space, the following accounts of other varieties of criminal activity in and around the city have had to be mostly restricted to the period since c.1800, but a few stories from before that date were impossible to resist. For one of these, on the magistrate Lister, I am indebted to the writings of John Styles. On the highwayman Nevison, memories and anecdotes arrive at random, in a mix of urban myth and social history, and for the oldest tale here, that of the Calverley murder in Shakespeare's time, the story touches on one of the great Elizabethan dramatic texts.

The typical scenario for the 'foul deeds' around Bradford might be seen in the brief but bloody tale of a robbery in 1851. In this, we have an example of a pattern of crime that will always be with us: a man foolishly walked alone on a January night, to visit his sick uncle out on Bradford Moor. William Marshall decided to walk these four miles, and on the way he met three ruffians; he was beaten up and left bleeding on the road. They took his watch and some cash. After telling him to lie still as a rock they ran off. But the victim had had a good look at one of them, a certain Alexander Preston, and there had been a glare from the Bowling Iron Works to help him make out the face. Marshall walked on to his uncle, his clothes ripped and his body bruised.

Police were soon on the trail of the robbers; a man called Raistrick had seen one of the men hiding a watch in a wall in the Spink Well tunnel; the talented lawyer Mr Deasley could do nothing to stop Preston being given ten years transportation. The story has all the features of a typical crime against the person in the nineteenth century and beyond: a rash act exposing the victim to assault; foolish actions by the perpetrators; no real investigation but a simple piece of local knowledge, and a dramatic trial.

This might be the staple commodity in the context of these Yorkshire stories, but there are also some other areas, difficult to include, but crimes that should be mentioned, as they are so significant in the Bradford conurbation. For instance, there is the Asian population and the changing nature of crime. I have included just one story (from the 1960s) with such a cultural and ethnic connection. I have omitted the phenomenon of the 'honour killing' which has been so prominent in the news in recent years. An example is the story of Tasleem Begum, killed by her brother-in-law in 1995. She had fallen in love with an Asian man while her husband was in Pakistan. She had met her lover while working in a Bradford supermarket.

The same could be said for the riots; the nation associates Bradford with street disturbances after the notorious riots of 1981 and the trial of The Bradford Twelve, and also for the later disturbances at the end of the twentieth century. I have left these out, as the events are seen as important for wider historical reasons. This can be seen in the literature spawned by the ethnic mix in the city: a vibrant, questioning and restless body of writing, represented by Tariq Mehmood's novel *While There is Light* (2002) which is set in Bradford and deals with the urban riots of 1981. Mehmood was one of the founders of the United Black Youth League.

Modern Bradford, then, certainly has its specific range of crimes, and some are related to ethnic tensions, but the emphasis here is on the crime of murder or other extreme crimes against the person, with other tales of affray, riot and sedition. One chapter here concerns the Yorkshire Ripper killings in the city in 1977–79.

What about the crimes that still lie cold in the records? Bradford has more than its share of these. Back in 1925 a correspondent wrote to *The Times* to complain abut the alarming number of unsolved murders apparent around the country. Another reader wrote in to list the few outstanding cold cases; there was just one in the West Riding – a Mrs Palgrave 'found unconscious with severe wounds on the head. She died without recovering consciousness.' The defender of the police then says, 'It does not follow that, because a murder is classed as undiscovered, the police do not know who committed the crime.' Unfortunately, by the 1960s, there were several unsolved murders around Bradford, if one includes Wharfedale and even as far as Skipton. I have dealt with some of these in my *Unsolved*

Yorkshire Murders (2004). But there is still some Bradfordian interest here.

This is why I have chosen to include three of these again in the present book: new thinking has emerged in the cases of Blum (1866), the Ripper (1888) and Hirst (1938). The city has had a more recent unsolved case too, but I have left this out of the main chapters. This is the Donna Healey murder. Her body was found on a building site in 1991, and she had not been seen since 1988. The investigation as to how she died still continues, and experts from Germany have been called in to help. There is some inexplicable connection between Bradford and unsolved or mysterious murders: the city gets more than its fair share. To a historian of crime, this is an added fascination in such a book as this.

But West Riding history has a high profile in terms of everyday, clumsy, almost perfunctory murder. There are countless tales such as that of the Keighley shoemaker who, in 1839, appears to have 'snapped' and as the *Leeds Intelligencer* reported, explained his crime (murdering his sister) in this way: 'I called her upstairs and said there were bugs behind my bed; she pulled off her shoes and got upon the bed; I then seized her and we had a struggle and I lost my knife; I ran and got another and with that I cut her throat ...' There are innumerable killings and assaults of this kind throughout the period c.1800–1950. It is not difficult to explain: after all, there was no understanding of mental illness for much of that time. Even in the mid-twentieth century, our state was still hanging people whose crimes were done in a state of mental derangement. But in places like Bradford, clearly the long hours of work, the heavy drinking, the poverty and other pressures on family life, all added to the stress that caused murderous aberrations in people.

Underpinning these stories is a miserable sequence of events in the criminal justice system in the nineteenth century, even for those who were not destined for the gallows. As the West Riding Justices *Accounts* for 1829–30 show, the end of the road for many was a trip to the prison hulks at places like Sheerness or Chatham; gaolers at Wakefield and Doncaster, for instance, were paid the huge sum of £117 to convey 146 people to the dock hulks. It is impossible to imagine a journey for some Bradford felons going from local gaol to Wakefield, then on to a ship in Goole, before going down to the Thames. Some unfortunates even went on carts to the docks. Such a one was Simon Hargreaves, a carpenter who was convicted of housebreaking and sentenced to life transportation in 1830; and James Moore, from Keighley, convicted at Bradford in 1833 for stealing a gold sovereign and a purse. He was given fourteen years in Van Dieman's Land.

There are also the interesting individuals who appear in these stories. One major player who is in the shadows is that of the hangman, and Bradford has its own famous son here: James Berry. He was a native of Heckmondwike, and had served as a police officer in Bradford before wandering into other trades (and a spell in the army), but later became the national executioner. He began this work in 1884 and wrote some memoirs, *My Experiences as an Executioner*. Other hangmen are of considerable interest too, such as the bungling Askern who caused agonising deaths for his unfortunate clients.

The prisons were busy and usually full around Yorkshire in the Victorian period, and criminals were easily created, as there were so many crimes on the statute book. James Burnley, the Bradford journalist, provides us with a few local statistics in this respect: he talks of the number of committals to Wakefield House of Correction between 1867 and 1873 being raised from 5,762 in the first year, to 7,425 in the latter. He notes, ' In the seven years thus accounted for, Bradford does not stand well. Burnley informs us that between 1867 and 1873 the committals in the Bradford district had increased from 882 to 1,411.

But James Berry almost provided me with a story for the book; this is because, after his career as hangman, when he was doing other things, he reached a personal crisis and was planning to kill himself by launching himself from the platform of the Midland Station. He was prevented from doing so by the intervention of fate, in the person of a preacher and evangelist who had, unbelievably, been 'told' to go to the station to help someone in need.

There is also a prominent history of politically-motivated violent crime in the city, and this came, principally, with the rise of Chartism in the 1830s and of the Luddites. I have left out the latter, again due to limited space, but included an account of the two high points of violent encounters in the fight for the working man's franchise. After all, the 'Physical Force' Chartist, Feargus O'Connor, was drilling troops on Woodhouse Moor, and Bradford itself was an epicentre of Chartist discontent. The narrative of these clashes in the streets was too dramatic to leave out.

Some of the most intriguing stories are available only as a brief memory, and we will never find the whole tale, as in this anecdote about Dufton Wright, father of the famous dialect scholar, Joseph Wright: 'Stories are told of his fame as a champion boxer among the navvies who worked on the Bramhope Tunnel: and of his great daring on one occasion when he captured a dangerous lunatic who had escaped control and taken refuge on top of a haystack.' Now, *that's* a Bradford story the historian would give a month's wages for.

Finally, I must thank various people who have helped in the work for this book, both personally and as authors who have provide me with indispensable sources. The publications of the Bradford Historical and Antiquarian Society have been very useful, notably John Styles' long essay on Samuel Lister of Little Horton. Thanks also to Brian Elliott, the Foul Deeds series editor, to the librarians in York and in Bradford, and to Andy Owens, Ian Dewhirst and the editors at *True Crime* magazine.

For permission to use some pictures from their collection, thanks also to Bradford Central Libraries, and to Carol Greenwood in particular.

CHAPTER 1

A Yorkshire Tragedy 1605

That spring Walter snapped.

In 1608 the play, *A Yorkshire Tragedy*, was published, and was printed as being written by William Shakespeare. Scholarship since then has shown that it was almost certainly not written by him. The story is in the popular Elizabethan genre of the domestic tragedy, and it is based on events at Calverley Hall, near Bradford, in 1605. These 'events' were a horrendous and bloody murder by a father of his own sons. He also stabbed his poor wife. It was a story with the same kind of melodramatic appeal as the Victorian sensational trial – full of violent rage and senseless blood-spilling, as in the work of a madman. It matched well with the current popularity for nasty and deranged Machiavellian revenge drama.

But there was just one minor but important difference: the events really happened, and to a family with links to some of the mightiest people in the land. The killer, Walter Calverley, had married Phillipa Brooke in 1599. She was a member of the Brooke family who included no less a person than Sir Robert Cecil; Phillipa was Cecil's aunt.

What actually happened that awful day in April 1605 we will almost certainly never know now. Walter had been in severe trouble with his mounting debts; he had been selling off much of his extensive land in the East Riding as well as property around his home in Pudsey, Burley and Menston. In fact, the couple had only been married for a year when the new husband was in prison for debt and was very ill. His mother-in-law had described him as 'unstayed' (unstable). There was a history of insanity in his family. His father, William, was undoubtedly a lunatic; he was a fervent Catholic at a time when that could

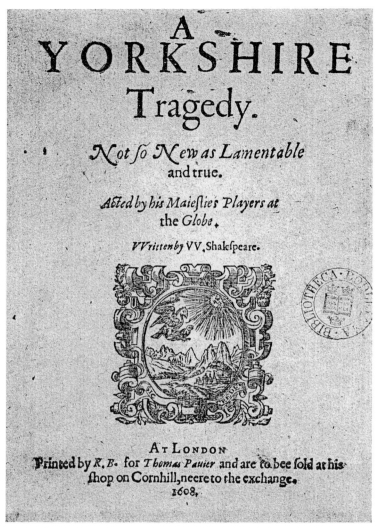

A Yorkshire Tragedy, *Quarto title-page, 1608.* Author's collection

have cost him his life, and at one time was imprisoned in London for making seditious speeches in public. He died at only the age of thirty-nine. The man had had huge fines imposed on him for absence from church, so the political and legal pressures were tight. It seems quite amazing that the Brookes allowed his son's marriage into their ranks at all.

The pressures from debt, religious belief and those of marriage to a powerful family no doubt weighed heavily on Walter. It would all have gone down very hard; the family could trace itself back to around 1100 when the Calverleys had come south from Scotland, and the place-name Calverley is mentioned in the *Domesday Book* of 1086 (meaning a clearing where calves are pastured). That spring, Walter snapped; there had been a catalyst, since there had been a notable witch trial in the area, just a month before he went into his rage. Locals had been spoken of with suspicion by other locals; it was all turning nasty.

What was there left for Walter Calverley and for his sons? His mind must have thought that death would release the boys from a life of penury and suffering. To make matters worse (and here we must read between the lines) his own mother, Katherine, who had lands around Burton Agnes, was buying more land and her wealth grew. She had said that she was not intending to leave any of this wealth to her stressed and unbalanced son.

The details we have of what happened at the hall come from a pamphlet published just a few weeks after the murders. Strangely, other legal documentation has not survived, and that seems more than coincidence when we realise that the Brookes were in bigger trouble: Lord Brooke was a friend of Sir Walter Raleigh, and he followed him into disgrace, being reprieved by James I in December 1603. The new king was looking for a 'good press' on his arrival from the north.

We rely for the narrative, then, on the pamphlet. This has him as a man under pressure from the start: a man ranting about his wife's infidelity. Then troubles come thick and fast, such as a report that his brother is in gaol, and that is the last straw. One poor son comes on stage with a whip and top and is promptly

Woodcut image from an early edition.
Author's collection

stabbed. Then he loses control totally and raves into his wife's room. In a desperate struggle as his wife tries to fight him off the children, Walter stabs the other boy, and his wife. She falls down wounded and Walter runs to find the other son who is

Part of John Speed's map, 1602, showing (circled) Calverley. Author's collection.

also wounded. The language is equal to any popular thriller:

HUSBAND: *Comest thou between my fury to question me?*
SERVANT: *Were you the devil I would hold you, Sir.*
HUSBAND: *Hold me? Presumption, I'll undo thee for it!*
SERVANT: *Sblood! You have undone us all Sir.*

Walter is finally tracked down, dragged before the magistrate and taken to Wakefield (not York as there was a plague outbreak at the time). But later he was moved to York and kept there until the next Assize. We know just two bare facts about the outcome. First, that he was pressed to death on 5 August, and buried on the same day; and that he was buried in the grounds of St Mary's. We think immediately of the death of Margaret Clitheroe when we think of pressing as a method of execution: slow and barbarous in the extreme. The prisoner would be naked under a board and stones would be gradually put above to crush him.

Walter's wife married again, a few years later; she had three daughters, and she lived until 1613. Two entries in burial registers tell the bare story of the Yorkshire tragedy: the first says simply, '*Calverley, St. Wilfrid's 24 April 1605. Wllm. And Walter, sons of Walter Calverley Esq.*' The second is more explicit and powerful:

York, St. Mary's Castlegate 5 Aug. 1605
Walter Calverley executed for murthering unnaturally
Two of his own children the 23 April 1605
Was buried the said fifth of August

A C Cawley, the literary scholar, points out the lingering fascination about the case. As he notes, Calverley's reasons for remaining mute at the trial 'are not at all clear.' Refusing to plead actually protected his land and stock, because the assets were left in a trust, so they would not be lost when the owner committed a felony. Maybe Sir Walter was much more canny than he seemed, and in control of the situation. A simpler solution, as Cawley suggests, is that 'he may have been seeking the speediest way to end his life.' If so, then he certainly succeeded.

CHAPTER 2

Nevison the Highwayman (d.1684)

This was his last caper into the lawless dark valleys of West Yorkshire.

In 1699 a newspaper report gave the following details of a robbery: 'Last week, in the dusk of the evening, three highwaymen set upon a country farm … the farmer and his friend got two of the highwaymen down, but the third coming up, shot the farmer through and killed him ….' There is nothing romantic in this, yet the media still persist in making the Dick Turpin myth escapist, popular narrative. Dick is the archetypal Yorkshire gentleman of the road (in truth a rapist, killer and horse-stealer) but the county has another and he has entered the realm of myth.

This is William Nevison, a man most likely born in Wortley near Pontefract, and hanged in York in 1684. Most areas in Yorkshire like to 'claim' him as their own, notably in the burgeoning heritage industry, but what is not widely known is that there is a strong oral tradition that he was active around Gomersal and Hartshead, and his most well recounted deed here was a murder, when he shot the landlord of a public house near Batley.

Nevison's fame (or infamy) across the West Riding and also the South Yorkshire stretch of the Great North Road made him the subject of

Highwayman, from a seventeenth-century narrative. Laura Carter

ballads and apochryphal tales; there is a cutting at Castleford called Nevison's Leap and an inn was given his name. The song *Bold Nevison* has some patently untrue statements, such as:

I have never robbed no man of tuppence
and I've never done murder nor killed.
Though guilty I've been all my lifetime,
So gentlemen do as you please.

The main story on his life is supposedly the feat that won him the nickname, 'Swift Nick', was a ride north to his native county after a robbery at Gads Hill in Kent. He reputedly robbed a man there in 1676 and then made his escape on a bay mare, riding north at an incredibly fast pace, some say going from Kent to York in a day.

We know that Nevison's father was a steward at Wortley Hall and that his brother was a schoolmaster, and we know that the robber himself was married and had a daughter. His wife lived on to be 109 years old, dying in 1732. The oral tales pass on a complimentary view of Nevison, that he was tall and charming, and never used violence. The truth seems to be very different. A diary entry for 1727 recalls a memory of Nevison, saying he was living with a family called Skelton – gamekeepers at Wortley. It reads, 'At the same time there lived with this Skelton Nevison, who afterwards was an exciseman, but being out of his place, became a highwayman.'

That detail makes sense: that an exciseman would find an attraction in the wealth attainable and 'turn tables' to the wrong side of the law. Further investigation reveals that he began his criminal career early, stealing when he was only fourteen; James Sharpe, in his book, *Dick Turpin*, says: 'After being punished for stealing a silver spoon from his father, he stole ten pounds from his father and his horse, set off for London, cutting his horse and slitting its throat outside the capital in case he be suspected . . . .'

It is hard to believe that the robber who haunted the Leeds to Manchester Road around what is now Hartshead and the northern fringe of Mirfield was also once in service with the Duke of York at the siege of Dunkirk. Everything about him fits the description given him in the Victorian period when the

Robbers hanged at the crossroads, from an early illustration. Laura Carter

myths were fully generated: 'The Northern Claude Duval', as Duval was the most famous of the gentlemanly highwaymen, and as the man whose life was once spared by Royal clemency.

But there is a strange mix of ruthlessness and charming oral tradition in his activities south of Bradford in his last years before being caught at Sandal. He used to visit one of his girls at Royd Nook and would visit an old inn called the *King's Head* north of Mirfield; he would most likely make his way from that base onto the roadside and wait for the Manchester coach. It would be a good corridor to 'work', along what is now the M62 close to Hartshead. But the tale is told of him stopping at an inn in Batley while on these excursions, just to take a drink, and the landlord recognised him. The man raised the alarm, but Nevison was quick, and as the landlord came to tackle him as the robber was mounting his horse, the foolish man was shot and killed.

The alternative story has the events at an inn in Howley, and in this tale the landlord, Fletcher, tried to trap Nevison in an upstairs room but failed. According to Victorian antiquarians, there was once a field near Howley Hall with a small stone on which was written, 'Here Nevison killed Fletcher, 1684.'

This was his last caper into the lawless dark valleys of West Yorkshire. He was pursued and was finally tracked down and cornered at the *Three Houses Inn* at Sandal. Nevison was taken to York and hanged. He was captured by William Hardcastle, who was buried at Sandal church in 1696. Nevison had always had a reputation that placed him in the Robin Hood tradition, mainly due to Lord Macaulay's famous *History of England*, in which the great historian says that 'The great robber of the

Many of the places shown on this extract from Jeffrey's 1772 map would have been familiar to Nevison. Author's collection

YORKSHIRE NOTES AND QUERIES. 79

SANDAL CHURCH.

W. S. Banks, of Wakefield, in his "Walks in Yorkshire," 1872, gave the following description of Sandal Church:—

The church, dedicated to Saint Helen, stands picturesquely in the midst of the village, and although it has no striking peculiarity of style of detail, it is kept in good repair. It is cruciform, consisting of nave with aisles, transepts, chancel, with vestry on the north, and a chapel, burial place of the Watertons, of Walton Hall on the south. The tower rises from the intersection of the limbs of the cross, and has six musical bells, dated 1812. The windows of the west end and transepts, and two at the east

Woods, of Sandal, and Woodthorpe, Westmorelands. Allots; Gills of Kettlethorp, stated to be of the Gills of Carrhouse; Vaughans and Nortons of Kettlethorpe—the last three being connected by marriages. One of the monuments to a Gill, done by Bacon, representing a woman holding a medallion with three faces on it, is very pleasing.

Hawksworths and Jacksons also lie here, and several members of the Grice family, which was seated in Sandal for several centuries and matched with the best families in Yorkshire. Perhaps the most interesting tablet in the chancel is that to William Hardcastle, formerly of Laverton, and afterwards of Milnthorp, gentleman, who was buried there 1st October,

SANDAL CHURCH.

end, are late insertions, and are early decorated in style. The three peculiarly placed east windows are glazed with stained glass, representing the four Evangelists. The large east window of the Waterton Chapel is perpendicular, whilst the rest are debased. The pillars and high arches inside have been redressed—those that support the tower being bold and good Common pews and furniture occupy the floor of the church. Upon the font are the initials C.R., the date 1662, and the letters H.B. and R.D., initials of churchwardens probably. Many monuments are placed on the walls and the floor—in the north transept—to Pilkingtons, in the chancel to the Zouches, including the well-known doctor, who died in 1815, to

1696. The tablet says he died 29th September, 1695, but the year is wrong, as the parish register shows. The memorial was evidently not put up til years after his burial, for it records the deaths of his grandchildren, who died at subsequent dates. He was no doubt the William Hardcastle who captured Nevison, the highwayman. Another important memorial of the past, placed in the church before 1532 (probably between 1489 and that year), is the carving on two oak stall ends, now part of the pew adjoining the chancel screen on the north side of the nave, consisting of the Percy badge —a crescent and double manacle—differenced with a martlet; two shields, one on each stall end, the first bearing the quarterings of the

Sandal Church, where lies the man who caught Nevison, from an 1850 engraving. Author's collection

north of Yorkshire levied a quarterly tribute on all northern drovers, and in return not only spared them himself but protected them against all other thieves; that he demanded purses in the most courteous manner, and that he gave largely to the poor ....'

Where is the truth then? Nevison, like Turpin, was most likely little more than a desperate man who had been an outlaw most of his life; it makes sense that, after concentrating on the Castleford and Wakefield areas where most travellers north would be easy prey, he would have to move west. The oral tradition around West Yorkshire plainly makes Nevison exactly the type to appeal to the later myths: courting young women around the villages between south Bradford and Morley, and having his bolt-hole around Mirfield, where the myths and tales are most widely told in the older local memoirs. True or not, it will not do the Bradford area any harm to have its own Dick Turpin character leaving a trail of murder and romance behind him. His fame had even reached Lincolnshire in the form of his ballad, as Percy Grainger, hunting for folk songs, found that the singer Joseph Taylor of Brigg, knew the song in 1908. In the end, the tale may be as much of an 'urban myth' as that of the famous Spring-Heeled Jack who was supposed to haunt the London streets in the 1830s, 'a tall thin man enveloped in a long black cloak' said to be the offspring of the Devil.

CHAPTER 3

'Detective' Samuel Lister
1756

... a formidable man to have as an enemy.

Popular history books and the media have given us a general picture of the eighteenth century magistrate that tends to suggest an idle, over-fed and peremptory fellow, too keen to have the next meal, who put the felons inside to cool off. Perhaps this owes a lot to the novels of the time. But documents do indicate that a typical magistrate need not have stirred from a comfortable chair unless there was an extreme emergency such as a riot or imminent war.

But there was at least one exception to this in the Bradford and Halifax area between 1751 and 1769. This was Samuel Lister, a formidable man to have as an enemy, and unluckily for the men involved in the 'yellow trade' of coining and clipping at this time, and in the risky activity of forgery, he was more than capable of going out to make things happen, and to play detective when needed. Lister was based at Horton House, and he had been trained as an attorney, having thirteen years in that profession. He had to stop the legal practice if and when he took up the magistrate's post.

There was a family tradition behind this; his father had served on the bench for the West Riding, and as the area covering Bradford and Calderdale was vast, mostly wild and empty, and in the first stages of an industrial revolution, a magistrate was sure to be kept busy. At that time there were around 200 capital offences, and also plenty of lock-ups, stocks and houses of correction to keep the less serious offenders out of circulation for a while. In 1764, in the Halifax parish of Lister's area, there was most likely a population of approximately 40,000, and there was

Bradford in 1835. Bradford Metropolitan Libraries

no magistrate in local residence when Lister stepped into the role. Bradford had three justices in the 1750s. But we are dealing with a remarkable man here, one who was highly regarded by the Marquis of Rockingham, the outstanding legal figure for the West Riding, always busy at York Castle.

Lister had plenty to occupy him in the activities of thieves and robbers, and in this work he averaged about twenty-six sittings each year; but it was in the coining circuit that he really came out from the usual rôle he played to become a detective, out to get his man. The man in question was one William Wilkins, who had been arrested and brought to the court for not paying bills at various hostelries throughout the West Riding. He had been searched and interrogated and on his person were found letters, one with a Gloucester postmark, and more astonishingly, a promissory note for the huge sum of £1,100 – a massive fortune at that time.

Wilkins said that he was from a place called Painswick in Somerset; but the letters and notes he had were not actually

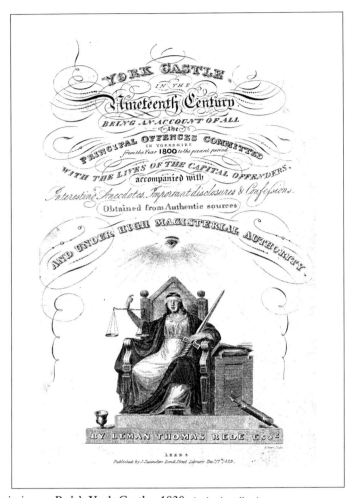

Frontispiece to Rede's York Castle, *1830.* Author's collection

signed by anyone of note. They were more than likely forgeries, and if guilty, he would hang. But the problem was: how to prove he was guilty? It was going to take extraordinary measures to achieve this, notably trying to communicate with the Painswick authorities, and this was something usually far too strenuous and time-consuming for your average magistrate to bother with. Not Samuel Lister, though; he was a determined man with a sense of challenge.

The first step was to enlist some qualified assistance, so he turned to a Leeds man, the Recorder, Richard Wilson. The two men decided to keep Wilkins locked up while information was gathered; they put items in London newspapers and sent messages to Gloucester. They were pushed for time: Wilkins was to appear at the Lent Assizes in the South West and in a quite short time. He could have had friends there to stand bail, as well, so they moved fast. This is where the alacrity of Lister in using the 'grapevine' around Bradford paid off, as one of his contacts knew of a West Country man visiting the town, a Walter Merrett. He told Lister to write to a clothier at Uley near Painswick, to ascertain information.

It was a triumph: 'Wilkins' was in fact one Edward Wilson from Painswick, wanted for forgery. It was soon sorted out then: Wilson was sent to trial at Gloucester on 20 March 1756 and was sentenced to death.

Lister also got to work against the clippers. This yellow trade involved filing or clipping coins down to an acceptable weight for local use, and so actually creating more coins with the clippings; it was very lucrative, and a capital offence. It was indeed high treason. The risks were high and it made the criminals act with desperation and resolve, even to the extent of murder, in the case of the exciseman, William Deighton, killed in Halifax in 1769. But the Bradford men still acted against the coiners, perhaps urged on by this murder. It was no easy task to work against the perpetrators though: the trade enjoyed considerable popular support. Lister was a part of this crusade to hit the coiners.

The best way to find out the villains was to employ *agents provocateurs*, and Lister, together with John Hustler in Bradford, did this successfully, their work leading to the arrest of two men on an inspector's evidence, and they were packed off to York Castle. He must have known the risks. Deighton had sent some men to York Castle, and he paid for it with his life.

But Samuel Lister was indeed a remarkable man. He saw the magistracy as something opening up opportunities to act on behalf not only of the law itself, and civil order, but as a means of reinforcing the authority in an economic context also. The

Bradford Court House. Laura Carter

action against the 'yellow trade' was done partly because he had links with local industrialists, and represented their interests, of course, in protecting the value of coins in trade circulation. His principal biographer, John Styles, appropriately quotes Lister's own words as explanation of his motives: 'I think it my duty not only as a magistrate but as a private person to do all that I am able to bring villains to justice.'

CHAPTER 4

The Haworth Gang
1817

... their particular forte was exploiting the old, the infirm and the weak.

A cursory glance at a map of the area around the west of Halifax, beyond King Cross, will show how many small hamlets between Warley and the Denholme or Wilsden districts would have been vulnerable to attack. In the early nineteenth century these were truly isolated communities, and the straggling small farms along the valleys were notably good hunting ground for thieves and robbers. It was also an age in which the benefits to criminals of having a good deal of support were obvious. In other words, put together this territory and a gang of ruthless men and you have mayhem and fear.

That was the case with the reign of the Farrar brothers, and their particular forte was exploiting the old, the infirm and the weak. They became known as part of the Howarth gang, and the three brothers, Isaac, Joseph and John, did some nasty and very low deeds before they were finally brought to court. What did finally stop them was a robbery so violent and yet so clumsy that it is hard to believe they were not out of their minds when they did it. The robbery

Footpad at the Haworth gang era from Rede's York Castle. Author's collection.

was a bungled attack on an old couple, James and Betty Heap. Everything about this attack was inept and singularly clumsy, as if they had reached the reckless stage of criminality.

James Heap was eighty-eight years old when the attack took place. He was too weak to go to court, but his wife made a long and detailed statement, and witnesses had been gathered. As the story unfolded in court, it must have seemed like a bizarre kind of comedy, were it not for the brutality involved, because the brothers had blackened their faces with soot, and this was coming off, even shortly after they burst into the Heap's house at Cold Edge. Betty had reported: 'We retired to our rest ... a little after nine o'clock .... Some time in the night I was awakened by a loud crash, occasioned by the door of the house being forced off its hinges.'

No firearms were pointed at the couple, but Betty was hit with a stick and told to lie down; the couple were in bed as the robbers came in. Betty had jumped up to dress, but was pushed into the bed again. As the Farrars started trying to light a fire by burning papers, Betty recognised Isaac Farrar, whom she had known since she was just a girl. The soot had not disguised him at all. The gang then started turning the place over to find any stash of money that might be there; it seems like they expected to find some. They were clearly a terrible threat, and terrified the old couple; at one point Betty begged them to leave if they would accept £100. It didn't do any good, and they cleared the house of virtually everything inside.

The gang stopped the (long-cased) clock but Betty guessed that they were in the house for longer than an hour, and at the break of day they were gone. But this has to be one of the most pointless robberies ever done: Betty eventually had all her goods returned and she noted that the only thing wrong with the materials was that some blankets were mildewed. After the events, and Betty's being sure that the men were the Howarth Farrars, a cluster of witnesses came forward.

There was Ellen Shackleton, who had seen the men out on the road on the night of the attack; two of the men had run into a field on seeing her. This was two miles north of the Heap's house. James Bradley was walking to the Farrar's house on that night, and he saw that when the Farrars were only twenty yards in front of him, they turned and ran sharply over a fence into a field. He actually ran after them (as he was with two friends) and verified that they were the Farrar brothers; he had known them for years. Joe Sunderland saw them close to that place, as he was going towards a drift mine. He saw John Farrar down the entrance to the mine, tying an apron; they had stored stolen goods inside. A man called Ogden saw an ironing cloth there. This turned out to be one of the items stolen from the Heap house.

Justice Bailey was not at all convinced by a motley crew of wastrels brought in to give alibis for the gang, and he passed the death sentence on them, but thought that there would be mercy shown, and indeed they were eventually transported. A writer of the time noted that the gang showed 'the utmost coolness' and that 'this calmness in the perpetration of crime could only be obtained by repeated practice.' So it was indeed, as the judge had pointed out that they had been before the assizes previously on similar charges, and that is why the death sentence was initially passed on them.

In this way at least some of the Howarth gang were removed from their patch, where they plundered the weak and defenceless.

The Black Bull, *Howarth: a haunt of the gang.* Laura Carter

CHAPTER 5

A Murderous Publican 1820

The sight downstairs was truly horrible ...

Bradford publican, William Oldfield, must have lived in the centre of a hellish maelstrom of anger, hatred and violence. Nothing in the world seemed right for him, and in particular the women in his life. He married young, and he had a family then, but this never worked out well, and he eventually married again. His first family and his new wife were at loggerheads, with Oldfield in the middle, and events occurred here that led to him being in court on a charge of killing his second wife. This is what happened that led to such a horrendous outcome.

Oldfield was landlord of the *Horse and Groom*, and according to a witness at the trial, William Wheatley, when he went to bed on 27 June 1820 he was woken up by a noisy man who thought he was the waiter, and he wanted drink. In fact, there were two staircases, one leading to Oldfield's quarters, and another to his guests' rooms. Just after Wheatley tried to get back to sleep he heard yells of 'Murder!' cried out by a woman's voice, and he assumed that this was Oldfield's wife, Mary, as it seemed to come from the landlord's part of the inn.

It was well-known by everyone that Oldfield beat his wife, and the poor man was concerned for her. But it was a case of 'cry wolf' at first, because of the familiarity of violence in the place. He said everything went quiet and he eventually slept.

Early the next morning, Wheatley had a terrible shock, as he went downstairs and found Mary's body. She was bloody, and strangely, her head was set backwards in a chair-frame. She was lying on the floor by the stairs. Trying to raise the house,

Wheatley ran upstairs to Oldfield and roused him with the awful words that his wife was dead. Oldfield's door was locked and his voice from behind the door said, 'How can I help it . . . a damned infernal bitch!'

The sight downstairs was truly horrible: bloody footprints from the hall to the kitchen; smaller footprints suggesting they belonged to Mary, and one or two men's prints. William's son, Ben's prints, were also there.

The Deputy Constable of Bradford, John Gibson, arrived at the scene an hour or so later, and repeated Wheatley's story, adding that there had obviously been a rough and unsuccessful attempt to try to clean up the blood on the floor. Gibson made it clear that, confirming that there was no mystery here, footprints led from the body to Oldfield's upstairs door. There was no call for any forensic genius to sort this out.

When it came to the medical report, the extreme brutality of the killing became clear: a Bradford surgeon, Dr Sharp, outlined the nasty scenario of the woman being severely beaten and covered in bruises, and that a cerebral haemorrhage had caused her death. There was a little doubt about whether or not she had suffered a heavy blow to the head, or perhaps suffered a fit (she was known to be a drinker and this was seen as a possible factor). He was also not dismissive of the fact that her worst wound could have been caused by a fall.

What was Oldfield's story? He said he had spent the day in Halifax and had come home around midnight, to find Mary in bed and very drunk; one of their children was lying there with her. His story was that he tried to get her out of bed and onto her feet, but that in doing this, she fell to the floor, and that he saw her walk very unsteadily out of the room and down the stairs. Other witnesses said that Mary had been very drunk that

York Castle. Laura Carter

evening; but counter to the drunken fall story was a statement by a servant that she had washed very bloody stockings belonging to Mary. How could a fall cause so much blood? The outcome of the trial was going to depend on two key questions put to Wheatley, as he was called to stand in the witness box yet again.

Was Mary's head resting against the front of the chair, and was the chair in the middle of the room or against a wall? He answered that the chair was against the wall and that the dead woman's head was propped against the front bar. It looked as though she had been beaten and hit the chair as she fell for the last time. That was the judge's thinking, and he passed a sentence of death. But there was high drama still to come.

The doctor wrote a letter to the judge a day after this sentence, stating that he was sure the death had been caused by a fall, and that Oldfield had not followed Mary into the kitchen to attack her. Justice Park signed a form of reprieve. In York Castle, the chaplain was given the letter, and the distraught Oldfield was led out of the miserable condemned cell to face what everyone thought would be a long stretch in Van Dieman's Land. But surprisingly, a month later it was decided that his sentence would be two years in York Castle. It had been an object lesson in the uncertainties of testimony, the bias of witnesses and the element of sheer good or ill luck in these affairs: the cases in which there was already a history of violence and where the general public would easily assume that murder was the natural progression from beatings and rows.

At this time York Castle was straining with its inmate population, and in 1824 work was begun on a new prison. Men like Oldfield, innocent or guilty, were swelling the ranks of prisoners at a time of general lawlessness.

CHAPTER 6

A Murder at Home
1824

He spoke a few words in seven years . . .

It reads like such a simple, uncomplicated statement of a killing: 'York Assizes: Abraham Bairstan, aged sixty, was put to the bar, charged with the wilful murder of Sarah Bairstan his wife, in the parish of Bradford.' In the busy, overworked courts of the Regency, dealing with new and often puzzling crimes from the labouring classes in the fast-growing towns, it was maybe just another 'domestic' that went too far. But this is far from the truth, and the Bairstan case gives us an insight into the plight of those unfortunate people at the time who were victims of ignorance as well as of illness. In this instance it was an awful, anguished mental illness that played a major part in this murder.

When the turnkey brought Bairstan into the court he commented that he had not heard the prisoner say a word since he was brought to York and locked up. This was nothing new to the man's family. Mr Baron Hullock, presiding, was shocked but also full of that natural curiosity of someone who just does not understand something. He pressed the gaoler to explain. He asked if the man in the dock understood the spoken word, and the answer was no. He also ascertained that Bairstan appeared to have no response to any sound whatsoever, nor any movement.

It makes painful reading in the court report to note that the prisoner was a 'dull and heavy looking man who . . . cast a vacant glance around the court.' The reporter in 1824 noted that the man 'appeared totally insensible of the nature of the proceedings.'

Poor Hullock had a real challenge to try to communicate with the man, trying his best to make the prisoner make any sound at all, asking several questions but receiving no answer. When he asked 'Do you hear what I say to you?' Bairstan simply stared at the officer next to him.

It was obviously going to be one of those trials at which many people were thinking that this silence was the best ruse if a man wanted to avoid the rope. The judge had to instruct the jury about potential fraud and the possibility that this was a tough and amoral killer with a canny wit and impressive acting skills. In legal jargon, the point was, was the man standing there fraudulently, wilfully and obstinately, or 'by the act and providence of God?' It was going to be a hard task, one might think, but not so: enter his sons and a close friend. They told a very sad story, and an astounding one, given that Bairstan managed to marry and raise a family.

His friend stated that he had known the prisoner for over fifty years, and that he was sure that ten years had passed since Bairstan had fallen silent. He explained that his two sons had been looking after the old man in that time. His key statement was that 'While he was sane, his wife and he had lived together very comfortably.' The man, Jeremiah Hailey, added that his friend had been capable of merely saying yes or no, and that the last time he had heard the man speak was when he had asked him if he knew his friend Jeremiah. 'He said aye, but I think he did not know me.'

Bairstan's two sons confirmed that their father had been silent in that ten-year period, only excepting one or two words. Henry said that since being locked up, his father had been pressed to speak and had answered something sounding like. 'Be quiet ... be quiet'. The other son, Joseph, confirmed that his father had been 'out of his mind' for ten years.'

There had been enough in him to marry and earn a living, but we must see with hindsight and more relevant knowledge, that Abraham Bairstan had been struck by a paralysis, perhaps combined with a depressive mental illness. In 1824, the most meaningful explanation was to put it down to God's Will, so the jury found that the prisoner stood mute 'by the visitation of God.'

Or, if one is pressed to say that it had all been a wonderfully impressive family performance, then would not this be the sure way to keep the old man from the noose? On the other hand, he was destined to be shut away for ever in awful conditions, being criminally insane. The truth will perhaps never now be known.

CHAPTER 7

Guns and Bayonets
1839–40

Something nasty was brewing and the law employed spies . . .

In 1840, W. J. Williams produced a report on prisoners in York Castle who had taken part in the Bradford Chartist rising. One man, Emanuel Hutton, aged twenty-eight, had been sentenced to eighteen months hard labour in Wakefield gaol. He was a woolcomber, and his condition was described as 'much distressed.' Williams reported that Hutton was aware that there had been a movement known as the 'Physical Force' Chartists, and it seems that he read the radical newspapers and had been on the margin of events.

The prisoner told how he had joined a crowd, not really knowing what was happening, and was led into trouble: 'I saw a man who told me to follow him . . . I saw a lot of men who bade me go into the market place with them – one gave me the gun.' The hard fact is that in the year building up to the risings in South Wales and then in Lancashire and Yorkshire at this time, many of the plans conceived had involved a desire to murder police officers. On Woodhouse Moor in nearby Leeds, Feargus O'Connor, leader of the 'Physical Force' men, had been drilling his forces. It was a national emergency, all based on the widespread political exclusion of the working men. O'Connor had been a well-known figure in this context around Yorkshire for some time, having done his first northern lecture tour in 1835. He had then published his newspaper, *The Northern Star*, in Leeds, from July 1837.

The Chartists wanted reform of the suffrage; the 1832 Reform Act had excluded those who were working with their hands in the toughest occupations that were making the Industrial

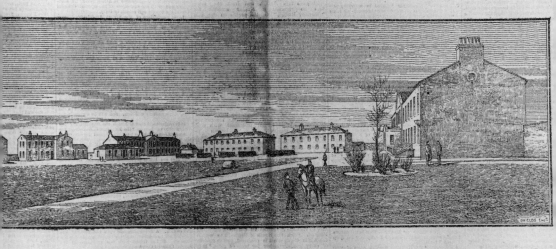

Bradford Moor Barracks in 1888. Bradford Weekly News, Bradford Metropolitan Libraries

Revolution possible; the Bradford woolcombers were a significant part of that deprivation, and they were fertile ground for the demagogues, and indeed for those who thought violence was the best way to achieve results.

The preparations for a full-scale confrontation with the forces of law had been on a terrifying level of agitation and fear, as the authorities saw it. In 1839, the wide space of Hartshead Moor, or Peep Green as it then was, was the scene of one of the largest Chartist rallies of the time. The area was like a fair, with over 100 huts put up for the sale of food and drink. Some said that 500,000 people had turned up, but a more realistic figure was perhaps 200,000. This was on 18 October, and O'Connor was there, talking about the death of tyrants; another leader, Bussey, insisted that the best thing Bradford men could do was buy guns. Hartshead had been in use before, back in May, 1837, when it staged a Poor Law meeting. It was fast becoming a spot in Bradford with a disturbing reputation for the local agencies of law.

Men did listen to Bussey, and they went to arm themselves. Justices of the Peace started taking depositions from shopkeepers who had had visits from desperate men out to use rifles;

William Egan, a Bradford gunsmith, recalled how he had had visits from such locals. He stated, later when he was a witness: '. . . a person whom I did not know and who appeared to be in the capacity of a labourer called at my shop and asked me if I had any guns or bayonets by me, to which I answered that I had not.' Pressure was being exerted; men were desperate to arm and to take on the local authority. Egan said that in one period of about ten days, he 'had been applied to in order to alter muskets which have been brought to me without the stocks . . . .'

Something nasty was brewing and the law employed spies – *agents provocateurs* – to infiltrate the radical activists. It was beginning to look as though Bradford would be the centre of a massive revolt of the excluded and oppressed people. James Harrison was an informer of this kind. In December 1839 he gave an account of what was going on with the extremists. He had been to a meeting at the *Queen's Head*, four miles from the city centre, and there he heard that there were around 260 men armed and ready. There was also a London Chartist at this meeting, and Harrison must have been worried. He recalled: 'In the bar there was this delegate, George Flinn, two men from the *Queen's Head* and myself. The man from London looked earnestly at me and asked Flinn if he knew me. Flinn said he had known me for three years and I was as good as any man in the room . . . .'

The magistrates were frightened, and wrote to the Home Secretary, expressing their concerns. These were E C Lister of Manningham, Matthew Thompson, H W Hird and W R Stansfield. They wrote about 'violent harangues of evil disposed and Revolutionary speakers' and they felt that 'some violent outrage' was about to take place.

What did actually happen in 1840? The leader of the abortive revolt was Robert Peddie,

Ebenezer Elliott, the poet and radical.
Laura Carter

Baron Rolfe, who tried O'Connor, from an 1843 print. Author's collection

and his narrative explains most things that took place. The plans of Peddie and his peers must have been terrifying to the place: Bradford then had a population of 66,000 and a police force of half a dozen men. There was no real police force outside London, and these events took place only ten years after Peel's first Police Act. It is no wonder that localities relied on the army in these situations, so naturally a bunch of ordinary labouring men would have no chance of success, and this was the case with Peddie's plans. James Harrison outlined Peddie's notions of a co-ordinated revolt, involving miners as well as the Bradford people. Harrison met with a group of insurgents at the *Junction Tavern* on Leeds New Road, and the plan was to go Leeds and set fire to the magazine. Peddie's talk certainly included the desire to achieve the Chartists' aims – universal suffrage, no qualification for voting rights and so on. But there was another agenda, feeding other, nefarious discontents as well.

Everything was nipped in the bud; plans and leaders were known. Major General Charles Napier was given command of what was then called the Northern District in 1839. He soon had men billeted around the West Riding conurbation – for instance forty-two men in Halifax in forty-two houses; altogether in Yorkshire he had a thousand troops. He had to act quickly; very extreme things were happening, such as a book in circulation in Halifax about facing barricades and how to face cavalry with a pike.

Peddie was given three years' imprisonment after the Chartist Trials of March 1840. O'Connor had stolen the limelight, and his trial was extremely protracted. In the end, no policemen

The Northern Star, *O'Connor's Chartist newspaper, 1843.* Bradford Metropolitan Libraries

THE TRIAL

OF

FEARGUS O'CONNOR, ESQ.,

(BARRISTER-AT-LAW,)

AND FIFTY-EIGHT OTHERS,

AT LANCASTER,

ON A

CHARGE OF SEDITION, CONSPIRACY, TUMULT, AND RIOT.

MANCHESTER:
ABEL HEYWOOD, 58, OLDHAM-STREET.
LONDON:
JOHN CLEAVE, 1, SHOE-LANE, FLEET-STREET,
AND ALL BOOKSELLERS AND NEWS-VENDERS IN TOWN AND COUNTRY.

1843.

Trial pamphlet of O'Connor's Lancaster hearing, 1843 edition. Author's collection

were killed in the streets, but that was soon to come, just eight years later. D G Wright has noted that Peddie's colourful radical career made him enemies on his own side of the law, too. Wright says that at one point 'The Scots Chartists decided they had had enough of this wilful, self-centred and histrionic man ....'

CHAPTER 8

A Killing at the Orange Parade 1844

... a relentless and furious attack ...

In the heart of a series of terrible outrages against ordinary people in Ireland, the year 1792 saw the foundation of the Orange Order. The loyal Protestants of the north of Ireland split the nationalist phalanx. That organisation would prove to be the focus for a horrendous killing in Bradford in the early Victorian period: the death and public fight had nothing to do with the Order as such: it was simply part of an ongoing antagonism in general, and Bradford happened to be a place where many Irish had settled. This confrontation led to five people being charged with manslaughter.

Behind this unpleasant and vicious attack was a contentious area of social history: the nature of the Irish communities in the fast-growing Northern towns. There were very large numbers of immigrants, of course, coming across to Lancashire and Yorkshire to work in the textile industries. Social segregation naturally meant a process of ghetto-creation, such as the area of Manchester known as 'Little Ireland' near the River Medlock. There were 34,000 Irish in the city in 1841. In fact Bradford had a much larger Irish population than Leeds, for instance, and that cultural presence was marked in the mid-Victorian period.

The cultural and political dissensions and divisions of course came with the immigrants. The general population knew that the Irish worked hard and had built most of the roads and railways, but the image was unkindly and harshly insulting, as in

Street Band, 1890. Bradford Metropolitan Libraries

the appearance of Irish people in *Punch* sketches and satires. The events of 1844 would do little to counteract this negative image: an everyday march turned into something quite savage in the streets of Bradford.

It began with the members of the Calverley and Greengates Brass Band holding the Orange Day parade and moving in procession through High Street, dressed in all the regalia of that order. As with all the garlanded parades of that era, happening every week, they carried flags and banners as they walked. Their repertoire for the most part was quite general and innocuous, but towards the end of the set they began to play the melodies of *The Boyne Water* and *Croppies Lie Down*. Now, the very word 'croppy' is almost always going to be potentially something to incite trouble. The song was always linked to the Orange yeomanry in the year of terrible repression in Ireland, 1798, referring to the vogue of cropping the hair short, in a mimicking of the French Republicans. The words of the song include a direct affront to these people:

Oh Croppies ye'd better be quiet and still
Ye shan't have your liberty, do what ye will,
As long as salt water is found in the deep,
Our foot on the neck of the croppy we'll keep.

The Irish watching the march began to make a row and hoot at the marchers, in derision. But the band went on and eventually arrived at their lodge rooms. But the matter was far from finished. A band of thugs had waited for the right time to get some satisfaction after this provocation (as they saw it) and they had hung around until some band members dispersed and set off home. At about eight that night the bandsmen were followed home, and in Eccleshall Road, near Airedale College, they were attacked. The drum was ruined, and then the musicians were set about and severely beaten up. The assault happened quickly and took place ruthlessly, the villains running into the night leaving a band member lying on the roadside, bleeding and mortally injured. He was badly cut and his head was bleeding profusely.

This unfortunate was one Benjamin Gott, and he died the next day, his skull fractured. It emerged later that the poor man had been hit by a cobble-stone. It had been a relentless and furious attack by a rabid gang, on unarmed and de-fenceless people.

Five men were tried for the attack initially, and later four more men from Keighley. The first group were found guilty of manslaughter and transported. Prison sentences were given to the second group, and the whole affair

A common view of the Irish at the time.
Punch

was assessed and understood as what we might now call an 'isolated incident' but with hindsight and some more historical reference, it is not difficult to see this as indicative of a deeper malaise, and one that has never really gone away. The general image of fear and mistrust in this period regarding Irish activities was never really eased, and such things as Arthur O'Connor's sensational act of confronting Queen Victoria with an unloaded pistol as she stepped down from a carriage near Buckingham Palace did not help to remove this bad press.

As for the general appeal of belonging to a brass band in Bradford, that did not diminish; as Gary Firth comments with regard to a photograph of a street band: 'They were big on volume and 'oompah' jollity.' As old films and photographs constantly remind us, the street life of Yorkshire towns at this time was as noisy, vital and appealing as anything in Shakespeare's London.

St George's Hall – the brass band tradition lives on. The author's collection

CHAPTER 9

Bradford Blamed for Police Killing 1848

There were plenty of witnesses to the attack.

In all the history books, 1848 is known as 'The Year of Revolutions.' In Italy, France and Germany, the middle classes, largely excluded from any say in political power structures, took to arms and there were battles in the streets. Britain could not help but be aware of these massive events. One of the most public and alarming British events of the year was the emergence of the Chartists yet again, in a massive rally on Kennington Common, which was to prove to be their last gambit.

The country feared a revolution of our own, and in London huge military forces were gathered and large numbers of special constables sworn in. Feargus O'Connor was once more prominent, being the overall leader this time, and the authorities expected some fiery speeches from him that would stir up trouble on a massive scale. But it was not to be. The government banned the procession and O'Connor, to his credit, persuaded the Chartists to disperse peacefully and go home. He then presented the petition to the government virtually on his own.

But word was out across the country, of course, that trouble was stirring again. The London rally was in April and, at the time, Manchester had been preparing for a march of miners by placing cannon in the streets. There was far less mayhem and riot across the land than was expected. But Bradford had a fiasco of its own, and a riot that took place in Ashton was

RATHER INCONSIDERATE

Policeman (suddenly, to street performer). "Now, then! just you move on, will yer?"

The policeman and the crowd, a Victorian view. Punch collection 1910

blamed by the press on Bradford. The event ended in murder and in a gang of men being tried for treasonable conspiracy. Because Bradford was the place with the most notable Chartist riot, it was blamed by the prestigious *Annual Register* for this killing. The headline suggested that the murder, which actually took place in Ashton, was part of the Bradford riot.

As the reports of the time put it, two men, Joseph Radcliff and Joseph Constantine, young men in their twenties and thirties, attacked Constable James Bright during 'the late Chartist and Confederate excitements in the North'. There were plenty of witnesses to the attack. People said they saw

Radcliff stabbing a pike into the officer's thigh. But Bright was also shot, and there was confusion as to whether or not the same man fired the shot that killed Bright. There was such a muddle over Constantine's part in the murder that there was no case against him on that particular charge. Radcliff escaped to America.

The trial of the other men took place in Ashton under Baron Alderson, and three were sentenced to transportation for life; two for transportation for ten years.

The killing was not in Bradford but the headline read 'Chartist Riot at Bradford – Murder of the Policeman.' What did then, actually happen in Bradford? There was trouble on two occasions in May, most marked on the 28–29 of the month. Rioters clashed with police; things turned very nasty, and eighteen people were charged with drilling and with having an intention to turn their guns on officers of the law. Some were given two-year sentences for riot and assembly; others were guilty of sedition. A massive crowd had gathered at Wilsden and marched 'in a military style' to the city. Early the next morning, with a strong military presence already in place, 100 special constables went to the Manchester Road area purposely to look for some arrests.

Two of the principal leaders of the crowd, David Lightowler and Isaac Jefferson were the targets for arrest. But when the constables reached Adelaide Street there was a reception committee – a massive crowd, ready for a fight. The centre of the city had been closed down and the expected trouble definitely came. The constables were on the receiving end, and suffered greatly. The yeomanry had moved into Bradford by this time. Some 200 infantry – bayonets fixed – set to work to intimidate, and the police drew their swords. *The Times* reported that '. . . the ranks of the civil power were thrown into confusion and disorder before the dragoons were brought up . . . .' In this confrontation alone, nineteen were arrested. The Riot Act was read.

In all this mass of violent history, it seems that the best way to understand what was going on is to look at individuals, such as the Irishman, George White. He claimed, just two years after the climactic events of 1848, that he had been in ten different prisons in his radical career. Looking at his part in Chartism, it becomes easier to see the causes of the antagonism. At this time, there were around 15,000 woolcombers who had Irish ancestry working in Bradford. There was a steady succession of strikes and complaints about the terrible living conditions of these people, mostly around the area of Bradford Beck. White was incensed at the lack of social betterment and any sign of the local authority helping in this plight. He saw the 'physical force' Chartist way as the answer, saying that he got 'a pike and a gun and hoped and trusted that every man would do the same.'

At the root of the anger and disillusion in Bradford was the plight of the handloom workers. Although there was some sympathy shown by the middle classes, when it came to physical force, attitudes changed. A severe economic slump was the foundation of much of the aggression, expressed with desperation and frustration. Chartism was a name and a platform that could front any number of varieties of unrest.

As Jools Duggleby has written, 'Bradford magistrates described White as a notorious Chartist ... and dangerous character,' picking out this one man from the larger picture helps us to understand who marched, who rioted and why. In many ways, Bradford was fortunate that things didn't go the same way that they did in Ashton, when the officer was cruelly cut down by the mob.

CHAPTER 10

The Lozenge Poisoning Case 1858

... how do you let people know they were likely to be nibbling sweets loaded with arsenic?

In November 1858 young James Archer was sent by his boss to bring some mixture used in the confection of sweet lozenges. The businessman who sent the boy, one Mr Neale of Shipley, had been earlier to the premises, and he had pointed out that one barrel in the store-room was the substance used – a mixture called 'daff' – and another, in a similar barrel, was arsenic. Clearly, this was a very important distinction to make. Daff was otherwise known as *terra alba* (literally, 'white earth') and was a form of plaster of paris.

James returned later to collect some daff, and the man who kept the store, a Mr Hodgson, was too ill to assist, so he sent the lad down to collect the material himself. James could see the barrels, but he could not see any label to tell him which was arsenic. The label was actually on the base, out of sight. But he saw a barrel of a white substance, and collected twelve pounds to take back to his master.

The lozenges were made by Neale and then sold on to local retailers. A few days later, fifteen local people were dead and many more seriously ill. Many of them had bought their lozenges from the Green Market on the Saturday night, just after they were made, from trader called Hardaker. As soon as the morning after, two deaths were reported – both children: Elijah Wright (nine) and Joseph Scott (fourteen). The result was complete panic in the streets. A speedy and massive police operation was put into place. It was a rare challenge: how did you let people know they were likely to be nibbling sweets

Old Kirkgate, from an 1850 engraving. Author's collection

loaded with arsenic? It was a simple matter to trace the lozenges from Hardaker to Neale, whose premises were in Manor Row (Stone Street); but the Chief Constable, Mr Leveratt, and Copland, the Superintendent, soon went to work in a desperately important communication exercise.

All available officers set about walking the streets to warn everyone they met on their normal beats; men set out with bells to announce the horrible accident, and bills were posted up, informing everyone passing about the deadly sweets. Hardaker still had thirty-six pounds of the stuff, and this was recovered. Townsfolk were bringing the deadly objects in to the law as time went on, but on Sunday there were over 100 cases reported of people suffering the ill effects.

The amazing thing is that, in the process of manufacture, no-one had suspected anything to be wrong. James Appleton had been close to the substances as they were mixed, and he had suffered severe sickness for eight hours as he worked with gum, sugar and peppermint, with the arsenic powder churning and spraying around him. Still, no-one thought to think about this unusual outcome in the process. There ought to have been some suspicion when Hardaker brought some of the sweets to Neale to point out that they were not the usual colour. He was given them at a discount for that reason, and the sales went forward. On sale, they sold at two ounces for three pence and the business was brisk.

The case came to court and Hodgson faced a charge of manslaughter through negligence. At the Court House, Bradford, Inspector Burnieston reported on going to investigate the room where the two barrels had been kept. The prosecution were going to have to prove gross negligence if there was to be a conviction. This means that there would have to be behaviour of a kind 'substantially worse than that of the average reasonable man.' An accused would have to be shown to have appreciated a certain risk he was taking in the conduct of his behaviour, rather than a kind of understandable thoughtlessness or error. The inspector realised that, following the actions of the young assistant, he could not see a label, and the weight of the barrel was 2 cwt. Similarly, the young man would not have seen the label. The crucially important detail then was that arsenic was coloured, mixed with a dye, rather than left its normal white colour.

All was clear then. James had been looking for a white substance and he had found it. His knowledge did not extend to an acquaintance with arsenic and its treatments or storage. Two medical men at the trial found very large quantities of arsenic in the lozenges. Each lozenge had about nine and a half grains of arsenic in it; this was more than enough to kill a person. But it must be said that there were other troublesome factors in this case, such as the finding of chromate of lead in the sweets under examination. There had been attempts to improve and regulate the manufacture of such sweets in Glasgow not long before this, and in that city there was, in 1858, a union formed to prevent the use of daff in the making of the lozenges.

The Arsenic Act of 1851 had not made it clear who actually were to be called 'pharmacists', to avoid the easy access to the poison by ordinary people, so anyone known as a druggist (like Hodgson) could store and sell the stuff.

The result of all this was a shocking death toll. As the trail went on at the Borough Court, inquests took place also, and in the end there were twenty deaths and more than 200 illnesses caused by this awful accidental negligence – but it was just that – not *gross* negligence. At the Assizes, before Mr Baron Watson, it was decided that there was no need for a jury; as everything said had shown that Hodgson had reminded his assistant about the arsenic. He had also shown the young man where the two barrels were placed. It was an unfortunate series of circumstances that led to many tragic deaths. The boy's testimony revealed an ignorance of all technical matters concerned. Hodgson would have to be acquitted of gross negligence, and in fact Baron Watson stated that he could see nothing that suggested negligence of any kind. As was confirmed in the summing up, Hodgson had 'warned his young man that the cask contained arsenic.' In the end it was simply that all would have been well if Neale had stirred from his bed and supervised the collection of the substance down in his storeroom. But that is with hindsight, and does nothing to alleviate the awful suffering caused by this.

If it had not been for the quick thinking and common sense of officers Leveratt and Copeland, the death toll could have been treble what it had been. As for the offending lozenges: the editor of a magazine several years later reported that he had some in his possession as dark mementos of one of Bradford's most horrendous poisoning cases.

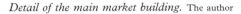

Detail of the main market building. The author

CHAPTER 11

Bradford Child Murders 1860

... *a thoroughly immoral man.*

Frederick Granhan had only been Chief Officer in Bradford for ten months when he met with a case that would have been horrible even by Victorian standards of child-murder. This was an era in which infanticide was so common that police officers would pick up corpses of children from dark street-corners and shady yards in much the way that they might collect a dead dog. It would not have been fully understood then, but puerperal psychosis, which led many women to kill their offspring, was certainly a factor; another reason for this common occurrence would of course be the shame of illegitimacy.

Women who killed their children in the nineteen century often went to asylums: about fifteen percent were treated in this way; there was a general leniency towards this version of the crime, although in 1865 the case of Esther Lack, who slit three of her children's throats, would make some re-think. Bradford had a similarly extreme case, just before the Lack murders, but in this instance, the killer was a man.

An eighteenth-century child-drowning case. Laura Carter

Inspector Granhan had to cope with a singularly unpleasant and awkward customer in John George Gowland. He was just twenty-five but with a complex, aggressive nature, and he constantly bombarded the bench with requests when first brought before a judge when remand was asked for. But in the hearing, before the Mayor of the city, Granhan had to explain that the man of mystery in the dock was either guilty of forgery or perjury. The officer explained that the man stood accused of killing his two children, and also the attempted murder of his wife, Mary. As they stood in court, she was fighting for her life in the infirmary, her wind-pipe severed and the doctors preying that no infection would set in and end her life.

Everything needed to explain about Gowland and what his status was rested on a marriage certificate; he was an attorney's clerk and seemed to enjoy being litigious and pig-headed. Before proceedings began he asked to say a word, and was told to be quiet until spoken to. He didn't like that.

The police officer then talked about the marriage certificate, and whether or not it might be forged. Gowland, at the first interview on arrest, had said that he was not married to Mary, yet a certificate issued in Durham in his possession said that John George Gowland had married one Mary Sutton of Bishopwearmouth, Sunderland. They had been married at St Oswald's, Durham. The date of the ceremony was given as 23 September 1855, and it had been signed by Henry Thomas Fox. Granhan said that married or not, the prisoner had been using this since arriving in Bradford. We must ask why? Clearly there were all kinds of benefits for a married man, so he could be 'married' when it suited him.

He had ruthlessly stabbed and killed his two children and Mary was due to follow. He was destined to hang, but at this point he was concerned that he must have bail. That was refused and so he then pleaded to be able to write to his mother. Granhan's statements were all about the despicable nature of the accused. He said he was a thoroughly immoral man; he would abuse any bail, and was likely to 'get out of the way.'

All the mystery man from Wearside could talk about was his letters. He asked if he could write to people to sort out proper food if he was to be locked up.

'You will have the prison diet, the same as other prisoners in gaol' said the judge. Then the inquest date was revised so that further examination on the children could be done. What did Gowland do? He complained.

There are questions to be asked. Why did he kill? It seems like a fit of insanity. The man was most likely severely mentally ill but there was no vocabulary then to describe him. It had been instigated by drink and he had reached for a knife. But the teasing question is whether or not this actually was his wife and family. There were plenty of Gowlands in County Durham at the time, and one of them raises an intriguing question. A George Gowland was born in Westgate in 1854, and he was the son of John Gowland and Mary Beadle. Mary was born in 1838, and that fits with Mary Sutton's given age at the trial.

Was Mary Sutton not married to Gowland? Were there things going on that added to the pressure of their having illegitimate children? After all, the man was an attorney's clerk, not a navvy or a labourer. If so, then the fit of violence and the murderous rage may well have been something from the last straw situation, a man under severe pressure, not only of drink and long working hours, but social stigma and almost certain financial hardship. The truth will never be known, and at the moment the story is just another domestic murder from an age when these things were very common in the new towns.

Westgate, where Gowland lived. The author

CHAPTER 12

The Hawkcliffe Toll-Bar Murder 1861

... he shot his wife in the back.

In past centuries, before a streamlined road system, a toll-bar was a dangerous place to occupy at times; arguments over fees due were common, and violence linked to this was always likely in some areas. There are a few Yorkshire murders which took place at toll-bars, and one of the most notorious was that at Hawkcliffe, north of Keighley.

In June 1861, below Whitley Head on the road towards Steeton, the toll-house was kept by John Holdsworth. He was originally a woolcomber but had taken up this lucrative but stressful trade and then married Elizabeth, and gradually things became difficult. He was not an easy man to live with, and the reason appears to be that he had a mental problem. In many homicide cases, there is commonly a reference to specific pains in the head before violence: sometimes this is described as an intolerable pain in a particular area. In the dialect of the time, the word then was a *gird* – a severe pain in the head.

Whatever the cause or reason, on this day in June, Elizabeth sent for her brother to come to her, obviously fearing he might do her and their son some harm. She knew the pattern and the danger signals before a crisis.

John was thirty-seven and he had been irritable and difficult for some time. This was known around the area, so when his brother-in-law, John Snowden, came, the neighbours would fear that something was brewing at the toll-house. Snowden was in for a rough time over that weekend. He was keeping watch, and prepared to play the 'minder' for his sister. But Holdsworth, even after going for a walk to his father at Silsden, was still not back to normal by the Monday afternoon, making it plain that he wanted Snowden out of his house.

The tale of the brutal conclusion to this 'lost weekend' for John Holdsworth appears to hinge on a small event that was the trigger to the man's final turn into insanity. A minor argument over fees with a Keighley merchant called Sugden started to add to the stress of the moment. Sugden went on his way, but Holdsworth was about to snap. What happened was that Elizabeth, whom her brother wanted to go away with him for safety, became the bone between the two terriers. Her brother, fearing for her safety and her husband becoming insanely possessive, shouted, 'Come back, lass, and let him go!'

The brother and sister took a little too long to walk away, and it was not a good move for John to threaten to bring in the law. Holdsworth had a gun and he shot his wife in the back. She fell to the ground, her body riddled with shot; John was shot too, but ran on, screaming for help. He had blood running down him, but ran on, like a man possessed. He had six wounds in him. There was a witness, a young man, and he had seen the shot fired.

The three days of hellish torment for the family ended with a chase over the moors. Holdsworth was seen running up the slope behind, and a constable, Miles Lister, went in pursuit. Another man, Joel Wright, was called in to help, and he was the one who found the gun: it was double-barrelled, and one had been fired. It is astounding to think that a civilian was allowed to go and touch, examine and interfere with a room packed with evidence as this was. When another officer came, he found that Wright had at least had the good sense to have the gun left elsewhere in safe keeping.

Lister had doggedly followed his man to the far side of Eastburn Crag on Steeton Moor, and tracked him to Aden, where his father lived. Holdsworth's words and behaviour when he was cornered were in keeping with his mental condition: he insisted at first that he should be hanged from a beam there and then to save time and trouble. There was going to be no problem to convict: he said, plainly, 'I have shot her.'

There was indeed a conviction, and for wilful murder, but at York Assizes it was clear that he was insane, and he was to be incarcerated for his natural life. Through modern eyes, this is a case in which the killer was in need of medical help, but there was none at that time for a man of his class and in his position. The Victorian years are brimming with annals of unfortunate people who took another life while in a state of mental distress, or while suffering from a chronic and severe mental illness. John Holdsworth was clearly one of these.

The road and the toll-bar were not particularly noted at the time; Black's *Guide to the County of Yorkshire* published in 1886 makes no reference to it, simply saying, 'The scenery increases in beauty as we approach.' The author was seemingly unaware of the dark history of the scene, and of a murder that occurred there just a few decades before his book was in print.

CHAPTER 13

The Year of Garotters and Robbers
1862

... the scoundrels then decamp and leave the victim on the ground writhing in agony ...

Up to 17 July 1862 there had been only fifteen robberies with violence in the city of London that year. But then a Member of Parliament, one Hugh Pilkington, was 'garotted' in Pall Mall. A new and terrifying crime against the person had been noted.

In its chronicle of November 1862, *The Annual Register* reported that there had been a 'garotte of terrorism' in London and in the provinces. The word 'garotte' was beginning to strike terror into ordinary people and newspapers were selling on headlines about this new version of street robbery. The report expresses the crime in this way:

> *For some years past there have been occasional instances of 'garotte robberies' – a method of highway plunder, which consists in one ruffian seizing an unsuspecting traveller by the neck and crushing in his throat, while another simultaneously rifles his pocket; the scoundrels then decamp, leaving their victim on the ground writhing in agony ...*

The popular magazine, *Punch*, covered the menace with its usual acuteness and dash; one cartoon shows some middle-class theatre-goers venturing out into the streets with a platoon of soldiers guarding them. It was nothing less than a reign of terror and it gradually became much more widespread than simply London's theatreland.

THE GAROTTER'S FRIEND

'Let go, Bill, can't yer–it's our kind non-interfering friend, Sir George Grey!!!'

One of dozens of satirical images from Punch *on the garotting panic of the early 1860s.* Author's collection

This 'modern peril of the streets' was first described graphically as 'putting the hug on' and it had its own jargon, the gang members having particular roles. First, the man called the *front stall*, a look-out; then the *back stall* who was going to grab the booty, and finally the *nasty man* who would move in from behind to take the victim's throat. At the time, it was seen as a variety of crime that was somehow not 'British' and journalists tried to blame it on foreigners. It was often written about in terms linked to activities by Italian mobs. But soon it was realised that this heinous crime was becoming a speciality of the new criminal underclass of the expanding towns across Victorian England.

The terror even entered the realms of popular song, with lines such as:

A gentleman's walking, perchance with a crutch
he'll suddenly stagger and totter;
don't think that the gentleman's taken too much
he's unluckily met a garotter . . . .

In the provinces the new crime began to take a hold towards the late summer of the year; 1862 was destined to become a proper *annus horribilis* for good people on the city streets, and northern towns were no exception. In Sheffield, one of the first notorious garotters outside London was Edward Hall, a man who was apprehended after a desperate struggle with police. It was reported at the time that he was 'the leader of a gang of ruffians who garotted and nearly murdered Mr Burnby, Earl Fitzwilliam's coal agent.' He was cornered and surrounded, then jumped from a high window in his home in Sheffield, to escape. But in Birmingham he was grabbed and almost killed by a huge police officer who punched the villain relentlessly until he gave in.

In Bradford, the Chief Police Officer, Frederick Granhan, was about to be busy with this new type of robbery and his constables' truncheons were going to be needed more than ever.

Characters like Hall began to appear in other parts of Yorkshire, and Bradford began to have its share of nasty street attacks by September of this year. The streets of the city and the suburbs were indeed perilous at this time. A man was severely bitten by a dog in Grafton Street; he almost had his leg amputated. A fishmonger in Keighley was robbed in broad daylight on his way back from a lunchtime tipple.

A more serious attack took place at Jerusalem in Thornton, where Joe Savile was attacked and robbed by two desperadoes who came across their victim at Well Heads. The attackers, James Jennings and William Shaw, showed no mercy; Jennings took the man's legs tight while Shaw grabbed his neck, then they ripped his coat off and somehow he fought free. As the poor man ran off the robbers shouted that they would catch him and 'kill him off'. Amazingly, though, the accused were acquitted because of lack of any clear accounts by witnesses.

Garotter gangs were not so lucky, and the full weight of the law fell on them. William Holes and James Lynas were in court for their garotte attack on William Dawson late on a Saturday night in Market Street. Dawson, an engine tenter, yelled for the police to help, and an officer came to the scene, to see the two robbers running away down Kirkgate. Holmes was trapped in an alley. Lynas was taken in Collier Gate by a detective called Milnes. They had taken a few shillings and a silk handkerchief. At York Assizes they were to pay dearly for that attack, with a long prison sentence and hard labour waiting for them.

In Calverley, on the moor, a Mr Summerscales was having his constitutional walk when he was set upon by two thugs called Elvidge and Hainsworth. They had used the established methods of one man behind to choke the victim while the other approached face to face, and they had taken his silver watch. But on this occasion, the victim could not positively identify the men and they lived to attack again.

Two hardened toughs called Lockwood and Murphy were one of the most successful garotting teams around Leeds and Bradford, and they became adept at the nefarious business; they had a cover as street hawkers, one selling oysters and the other sold nuts. They trod the streets around the whole conurbation, and were finally tracked down after an attack in Hunslet, though they had been active in Armley and Bingley. Murphy was the 'nasty man' and appears to have been extremely threatening and dangerous. It is not difficult to see how this crime would catch on in the criminal ranks; it reached the proportions of being a 'glamour' offence in that in took skill, a brazen attitude and a total lack of fear. Lockwood and Murphy almost beat their last victim to death, and they took a trip to York Assizes where they were due to suffer physical punishment and years inside.

The press began to speculate about how the most likely recruits to the garotting craze were 'ticket-of-leave men'. These were convicts whose terms of sentence had been lifted after good behaviour, so that they could go into society to work, thought they were required to attend musters, just as today

Examples of a Ticket-of-Leave, one was issued in Australia, given to a man after a set period of his sentence. Author's collection

we have a licence system in the current penal code. A ticket could be granted after the prisoner had served at least three years. Penal servitude had replaced the use of the prison hulks in the Thames estuary after 1853, and men who had only served three years of a seven-year sentence could be released under this scheme. Ordinary folk started talking about all criminals as 'ticket of leave men'. The popular journals enjoyed creating this moral panic, making their readers envisage the local streets filling up with desperate and hardened criminals waiting to strangle them as they strolled to the Sunday bandstand concert.

All this led to the passing of the Garotter's Act of 1863. In some quarters people raised a glass to the villains because their actions had introduced extreme and repressive punishments back into the criminal law. In Bradford, the vogue had been just a small part of the life of a very violent and brutal community. One way of seeing this is to note that, while thugs were robbing in the dark streets, hundreds of men were gathering to watch bare-knuckle fighting, as they did at Cottingley Cliffs when Laverty and Curlly fought on a Monday morning in this violent year. Two officers found the men fighting 'near the bottom of a small secluded nook near Cottingley Moor, the ground around rising up in the form of an amphitheatre'. There were six hundred people in the crowd, and the boxers were fighting for a prize of £10.

Everything about the city at this time suggests a community on the edge of reason and order; the womens' refuge had hundreds of clients and even the traditional mummers' plays turned violent when fists flew on the doorsteps of good, honest people as the mummers' demands for cash grew too impertinent. There was even a minor scandal when some mill owners found themselves in the dock at the Borough Court. But at least there was no violence there: Thomas and Jeremiah Hall of Shipley had merely stolen £100 in a warehouse scam.

The year 1862 was a year of living dangerously in most English cities. In London street crime was obviously at a peak of atrocious violence, but the north was certainly not exempt from this 'new crime.' As so often, *Punch* saw the heart of the matter, and in their cartoon, 'Jones is not afraid of his shadow' they summed up the nature of this particular fear. The little man with top hat and umbrella sees the giant shadow of a garotter with a huge club on a wall as he walks along. But the good citizen in the picture, ironically, carries a revolver.

CHAPTER 14

The James Waller Murder 1862

... almost 10,000 people had gathered to see Waller die.

Sometimes, the record of a crime comes down to us with more fascination in the social history of the execution of the condemned rather than in the crime, which in many cases is straightforward, with no psychological subtlety and with no scene of criminal complexity. Such a case is that of the murder of William Smith.

The killing was like so many others involving poacher and gamekeeper through the centuries. James Waller, a woolcomber, aged thirty-one, chose Bonfire Night 1861 as the time he would exact revenge on Smith the gamekeeper, a man who had defied and challenged him on more than one occasion. The scene was at Hawksworth Hall, Bingley, and a more uncomplicated crime would be hard to find. The servant of Timothy Horsfall of the Hall was merely doing his duty and it cost him his life.

Waller approached his victim in the evening with a double-barrelled shot gun. He turned and let the gamekeeper give chase, then stopped, turned and fired. Smith put his hand to his chest and said that he was done for. Then Waller shot again, directly into the man's chest. There appears to have been no great effort to avoid being recognised; it was a rash and desperate act but it gave the man some kind of twisted satisfaction to see his victim fall and die very quickly. Several people came to the noise of the fracas, and Waller, who had gone inside his own house, came out and pretended to be shocked, but

The Hawksworth coat of arms. Laura Carter

Smith was clinging desperately to life and said that Waller had shot him. Officers soon came to the area, but were unable to find Waller in the woodland tracks.

It took Smith (known familiarly as Davey) a long time to die. He finally took his last breath on Tuesday, almost two days later, at the Denby farm. The tale is so familiar: Waller had been before the local magistrates several times for poaching. Only a few months before he had been shooting at someone in the area and was fined. The first inquest was held at the *Angel Inn*, Baildon, and the jury were taken to see the corpse of the victim. A story emerged of the team of keepers that day being out to catch Waller, who was a constant nuisance. Another keeper heard the shots and saw a billycock hat that was almost certainly Waller's, from a distance through the woodland. Waller had been seen several times before the actual killing, shooting at game.

A Sergeant Inman of Otley said that he had been to search the Waller place and there he had found powder casks, and he said more about the long-standing feud between Smith and Waller. On two occasions the keeper had had Waller in court at Otley, and there had also been an assault on Smith done by Waller's son, for which he had been fined eight shillings. Inman said he heard Waller say that rather than go to court again he would 'blow the brains out' of Smith. There was not much subtlety here, and no worry that his enmity for Smith would be widely known. He was rash, bold and recklessly outspoken.

It was clear from witnesses that Waller had a deep, rankling hatred of Smith. It was said that many local men were scared of Waller, as one put it, 'as a toad is of thunder'. Poor Smith had to lie in agony while a surgeon took some pellets from his body. The surgeon was Mr Steel, and he gave testimony, as did the owner of the Hall, magistrate Timothy Horsfall. He had gone over to Lower Springs also, to see the dying man. Being the efficient local lawman, he took down the statement given by the victim, and in summary, this was that James Waller had been pursued towards his home, then turned and shot at the keeper. Smith had said he did not take the muzzle off his dog until he was shot. One William Davey was with poor Smith when he died, and he reported that the man had said over and over, that Waller had killed him. So it was an open and shut case.

The most telling witness was surely Ann Wilkinson, whose home Waller entered with a gun in his hand, looking for a spot from where he could see Smith. She saw him move away towards Lambert's farm at Sconce. Waller had quietly gone away while Ann was distracted. It was not going to be difficult to catch him, and it was just a matter of time before he was brought in by constables, after being found in a barn belonging to John Holmes at Eldwick. He was said to be 'pale and haggard and much reduced'. They took him to Keighley lock-up.

At the trial at York, Waller pleaded not guilty, but that was just a formality. It took very little time to condemn him. The jury took only twenty minutes to decide. When this was stated, Waller had no last words to say, and here we come upon a detailed account in the records of the process of confession and execution. This narrative was a common one in Victorian times, with this kind of literature having a great readership; writers reporting on the case tell us at great length what was said. The judge's speech is lengthy and moralistic. The heart of the summing-up was that the culprit had 'Wilfully taken away the life of this unfortunate man.' The black cap went on and the sentence was passed. Waller's story becomes no more than one more statistic in the long line of those hanged at York. A large

Turls Green Lock-up: something like the place the killer was first detained, from an 1850 engraving. Author's collection

number of people from the Bradford area had walked all night to arrive in time for the hanging. Reading between the lines, it is evident that the locals from Bingley and Otley were eager to see justice done on one who had taken away one of their own.

But otherwise the crowd was there for the entertainment. When his neck was stretched at mid-day, almost 10,000 people had gathered to see Waller die. This execution was done with a high level of ritual and ceremony: the Governor at York, William Gray, with the Under-Sheriff and two men of the cloth arrived with halberdmen to be present at the fatal hour. Waller knelt and spoke the Lord's Prayer.

It was all over at twelve. Earlier in the day Waller had talked about his victim, and also told the world that he had had two children who had died, and that he hoped he would meet them in Heaven in a very short while. His last words about Smith the gamekeeper were that he hoped '. . . there is no bad feeling between us now.' He had the temerity to say that he hoped to meet his victim in Heaven.

It took Waller two minutes to die on the end of the rope; this was over ten years before any professional executioner gave serious thought to the virtues of the 'long drop', which hastened death and offered a humane end to the lives of murderers.

CHAPTER 15

The Wife's Tragedy
1862

*She often had been in fear of her
life while living with him ...*

In today's enlightened times, we know about mental illness associated with puerperal depression. We know the patterns of depressive behaviour, the stresses upon young mothers, and the need for support and understanding. Not so in the lives of the working class people of Victorian Britain. The washing and mending still had to be done and the husband, after a long shift at the factory, would want his tea on the table.

Shamefully, in this context, beatings were also common, and the popular press of the cities where families often lived in jerry-built houses in warren-like areas, reported an endless series of stories about drunken men beating their wives. Bradford has one of the most heart-rending of all these stories in its annals of crime.

What doctors now call puerperal psychosis affects one in every 500 births. The incidence of suicidal urges is sometimes a part of this. In centuries past, the fear was that childbirth and the period of the first months of a child's life would be very precarious, and largely because of intentional infanticide. As early as 1649, in Garnet's *Book of Oaths*, a bishop or chancellor had to administer a set of oaths to midwives, and one of the statements made was: 'Item: you shall not suffer any woman's child to be murdered, maimed or otherwise hurt ...' There was general fear, then, when it came to the likelihood of infanticide.

But the woeful tale of Mary Ryan and her children is a most extreme case of the suicidal drive; she had rowed with her husband and he had struck her, and after walking aimlessly for a while, she and her two young children could not return to her husband. She told her mother that 'she durst not return to him in his lonely cellar any longer.' In the early evening of a September day in 1862, Mary drowned herself and her two children (the youngest being only nine months old) in a mill dam in Frederick Street.

They had stayed at her mother's (Bridget's) house on the Tuesday night after her husband had come home drunken and violent. Mary's friend Mary Costello ventured into the man's cellar and was allowed to take a child's chair and some pieces of cloth, to take to Mary. But the wife was in fear of her life and would not go anywhere near her home.

Mary's mother told the tale of her daughter arriving at her house on the Tuesday, one of her eyes black and suffering from intense pains in her back. He had kicked her. Mary had then gone to Ebenezer Court for a while, and talked of going to the workhouse, as there was no hope for her. The full tale of their unhappy life together emerged at court. She had often been in fear of her life while living with him, and just before the fatal day, her mother said, Mary had been given six pence by the man, but he had refused to let her take away a bed. He had raged that he was in debt and could do nothing until that was resolved. There was clearly no hope there: he was a drunkard.

Patrick Ryan had set off on Monday to obtain some materials and tools so he could find work as a tailor, which was his one-time trade; but he had met some drinking companions and they had settled down for a binge that lasted into the early hours of Tuesday. When he finally stumbled home, Patrick was ready for a fight. It was very one-sided; he came home by clambering through a window and was soon over the edge of reason. The trigger was that there was no food in the oven waiting for him. He woke his wife up and asked where his supper was? Mary said he could get it wherever he had been for a full day, and so the anger welled up in him.

Her husband said he hit her with the flat of his hand. He said that she started weeping, and to stop her he raised his right hand and said he would smack her again if she did not shut up. He relented and went to bed, his stomach empty.

Everything Mary did after that suggests a severe depression and extreme anxiety. She rose very early and cleaned the whole house thoroughly; then, as the argument simmered on, she washed and dressed her children, and walked out of the house. He had tried to cajole her back, going to Mrs Costello's and apparently trying to appease her. But at court, his attitude was revealed in its true light when he said, with a kind of twisted pride, that he had never hit her 'with a closed fist'.

It took the jury just fifteen minutes to come back in with a verdict of suicide but 'while of sound mind' and in a 'fit of passion.' Therefore they considered that there was a clear and sane intention to take life. The coroner said it was undoubtedly *felo de se* (literally, 'an evil-doer unto himself'), so this sorry affair ended, in legal terms, with a suicide and two murders, committed by a woman with a wilful intention. But the story of her inner life, of her bottomless suffering at the hands of a beast, never found a place in that court.

Mary Ryan, like so many distressed young mothers before her in the long history of desperate infanticide, found a pool the quickest way out, as the story of Elizabeth Chivers, back in 1712, had shown in *The Newgate Calendar.*

The Guard House Murder 1864

Sarah had been attacked brutally, her head very nearly severed . . .

Constable Henry Smith of Keighley stood in the dark of a barn, a place where he had been keeping watch over the corpse of Sarah Terry, and late that night he heard footsteps. The man he eventually saw lighting a match and eating bread and cheese was the main suspect responsible for Sarah's murder: her husband, Bryan. Constable Smith walked across and made the arrest. Terry could only say, 'It's a bad job. It cannot be undone now.'

The constable and his colleagues had been searching far and wide for the missing man for some considerable time, hunting in the fields and barns around Far Whin and West Bank. Reservoirs had been drained as well. The officers in charge expected a suicide following hard on the horrible murder of a wife. But instead, here was the missing man, ravenously hungry, back to his home, starved out of hiding.

Sarah had been attacked brutally, her head very nearly severed from her body. But this had not really come as a shock to Sarah Milner, a neighbour who had feared the worst for some time. The Terry family had been living with a violent father for some time. Sarah Milner had become a habitual carer for them, always looking out to help, and to be sure that Bryan was under control.

Earlier in the evening of this fateful day, the couple

Green House Farm. Laura Carter

had gone out to a barn to attend to a new-born calf. Sarah had seen them walk past her window. But they had not returned and she began to worry. When the Terry children came home, she learned that they had seen their father walking in a field, carrying a shovel. That was a detail with a menacing shadow over it: what had he been up to?

In Keighley lock-up, Superintendent William Gill Smith questioned Terry. He heard a gruesome and shocking tale: in the barn, as his wife was feeding a calf, Terry had cracked her across the skull and the neck with an iron bar. This was

William Gill Smith, investigating officer. Laura Carter

followed by a frenzied attack with a knife, cutting her face. He had run off in panic, taking the bar, knife, and also a spade, leaving his wife in a pool of blood.

Amazingly, after such a frenzy, he had run off onto the moors and dug himself a hole as if he were a hunted fox. He had the spade with him, and dug a hole from the back of a ditch, as a man might start some open-cast mining, then cowered there, squatting well within reach and hearing of the searching police officers. The place was checked out by another officer, and there the spade and bar were found. The knife, according to Terry, had been thrown into a beck.

Three days after the murder, the case had become a local sensation and ordinary folk went to stare at the 'fox-hole' and to wonder at the kind of animal who had been living amongst them. The trial was therefore going to be a high profile event for the media and for the general public. Sure enough, the crowd turned out in force to hear Terry and they were not disappointed, because he showed all the obvious signs of a man distracted and sadly gone in his wits, muttering nonsense and asking why he was there at all.

The magistrate was a neighbour, John Briggs, and he tried to be tactful and discrete; such a shocking case on his doorstep and in such a quiet place was almost too much to handle; he simply stated what his duty was, to commit the man to trial at

York Assizes. But what was the motive? The fact is that there was a track record here, going back to Terry's suspicions of an affair between his wife and her brother-in-law, James Spencer. Terry was a strong, aggressive and violent man; there had been a confrontation – a fist-fight – and this led to their appearance at Keighley Petty Sessions. But the actual immediate cause of the murder of his wife takes us in another direction.

Sarah Milner had heard Terry muttering as he had walked past her house on the way to the barn that night. Why this was so emerged later, and the cause of his discontent was an extra pound in a shared money-box. He had found an extra pound in that box, and he had no knowledge of where this had come from. When he went out to the barn where she was feeding the calf, she admitted that she had sold the calf. Terry knew nothing about this. He snapped. He had promised the animal to someone else, and he had been crossed, and by his own wife.

It had been one of the most bloody and repugnant killings that the Bradford area had ever known. The inquest involved medical statements from Dr Cockcroft and several other witness accounts of what had happened to poor Sarah. Her body had been 'weltering in blood' and the razor used had made a deep cut: the jugular was severed and even the bone was visible, so extreme was the injury. The crucially important detail established by the doctor was that he thought Terry to have been rational enough to have known what he had done. It looked as though York Castle was going to have another guest on the scaffold.

But this was not to be: his behaviour in court convinced the jury that he was not sane. He muttered and rocked to and fro, often weeping. After ten minutes discussion, they found him not guilty and not in possession of rational faculties: the sentence was to be life imprisonment. However, this dramatic story does not end with the killer languishing in a cell. On 28 April, after a visit from a Keighley surgeon and another man who were working to have legal documents signed, Terry took his own life, and all that was required for the task was a pair of leather garters. He had joined these together and hanged himself from a bar above a window. He had also gone through a pattern familiar to prison officers who have to be vigilant in such cases:

the process of self-harm before the successful suicide; in Terry's case, maiming himself with some nails he had obtained from somewhere.

Bryan Terry's corpse was brought back for burial in Keighley. His story had been one that easily outshone anything in the fiction of the Brontës (whose father was still alive and living close by at this time) in terms of its violent passion, but there was nothing at all romantic about Bryan Terry. His soul was surely as restless and tormented at that of Heathcliff: a malevolent presence around Keighley if ever there was one.

CHAPTER 17

The Violent 'Pluralist' 1871

Behind him lay a trail of emotional chaos ...

Robert Dalby liked the company of women. He liked them so much that he made a habit of marrying them. The fact that the English legal system dictated that one wife at a time is permissible, and not having several at one time, did not deter him. Dalby was fifty-six when he was finally tracked down and he stood in court in Bradford in this precariously illegal situation. He had four wives at that time.

This might all seem little more than a sad and farcical situation, but Dalby was also in the habit of using his fists against women. At the time of his arrest he was living in Cleckheaton and was sharing his home with Mary Copley, but he had three others, and the last of these was with Mary Ann Mortimer. It is in his life with this particular Mary that we learn about his nasty side. Dalby, only two months before his appearance in court for bigamy, had been charged with a violent assault on his first Mary.

The man had been two months in prison, and when he walked out again a free man, the officers were waiting for him with the more serious charge ready for him. After zealous enquiries around the area, it emerged that Dalby had married six times. Behind him lay a trail of emotional chaos; one of the women had died, and another had disappeared without trace. He was a man of mystery who had made a terrible mess of many who had the misfortune to meet him and to fall for his considerable charm.

He was ostensibly a schoolmaster by profession, so we have to assume that he found some time to earn a living, in between the time required for courting and setting up home with this succession of ladies. Police did ascertain the right documentary information about his current marriage when arrested: he had indeed married Mary Coley at Calverley in 1845. It must have taken a very long time to track down the other three who make up the total messy picture of the man's life, but they were all found and informed of the truth.

More recently, he had ventured into Lancashire where he would not be so well known, and presumably where he was less likely to run into former wives or even relatives of those wives. He married Mary Ann Roberts in Hulme, near Manchester, at Holy Trinity Church; he also wed Margaret Scholes at the parish church in Rochdale in 1865. Finally, within the last year before his arrest, and just months before settling down with his Mary at Cleckheaton, he had stood at the altar to become the husband of the Mary Copley he had taken to beating, and this was in Birstall, in August 1870. This is very difficult to absorb, but it covers most of the marriages.

Amazingly, Robert Dalby had lived for a while with all of these, and had children with them. There were Dalby children across the Pennines, and also scattered in Wales as well: this was to one Ann Roberts, and the pluralist, speaking in court to an awestruck array of listeners, referred to the Welsh wedding as 'The only honourable marriage of the lot.' In fact, when pressed to explain his behaviour with some semblance of meaning and sense, if that were possible, all he could say was that he had been spending years of his life doing little more than 'seeking an honourable woman to settle down with.'

The dark shadow beneath this ridiculous lifestyle was that of the pleasure he clearly took in striking and beating his women. Not only was there a trail of illegal alliances behind him, but also a number of young women who had felt the back of his hand. Another spell behind bars was waiting for him – this time for a considerably longer period. It is on record that all his former wives were tracked down and interviewed, and we can only imagine the stunned and alarmed reactions of so many women being told, in effect, that their children were bastards and their marriage certificates were invalid. They had all wondered where the husband had gone, why the money had stopped arriving, and who was going to feed and clothes the families.

There is no doubt that the rogue philanderer, Robert Dalby, spent no time worrying about these questions in his cell.

CHAPTER 18

The Sad Case of Liz Shepherd 1871

There were bloodstains on walls and on the stairs.

I f we examine the lives of prostitutes in the Victorian period, the extent of the risks they ran in their everyday lives is truly remarkable and often incredibly reckless and wrong-headed. In their trade, they had to inhabit not only the dark world of the industrial city on a smoggy evening, among beer-shops and inns, but in the daylight, when there was still custom, they adapted and tried to survive. Many failed, and such a one was Liz Shepherd. At just twenty-eight-years-old, she was working at any time when there might be clients, and her need for strong drink led to her death.

At three in the morning in May 1871, Liz fell from a high building at the junction of Manchester Road and Little Horton Lane. It was a quick death, as she slammed onto the asphalt and fractured her skull. Around midnight the night before, she had taken up with three young men, and one of them had suggested that they all go up to his workshop, a room on a very high level, and accessed by a long and cramped spiral staircase. They had

Liz Shepherd falls to her death. Laura Carter

planned a night of debauchery, and somehow carried a gallon of beer and a bottle of whisky with them, as one man, called Barraclough, said that the workshop would be a quiet and private place to enjoy themselves. He had the keys to the place, as he had formerly been employed as a wire-worker there.

The group, comprising Liz, Barraclough, Richard Gray and Harry Harte, soon felt the effects of the alcohol and things got out of hand. They had met Liz at the *Queen's Hotel* and knew her reputation. This was that she was not too choosy about the company she kept, and that when plied with liquor she was good entertainment. But the party became noisy, and a police officer called Bower, on his beat in the area, reached the yard near the base of the building and heard an altercation. A woman's voice screamed out something, and a man's voice in reply said, 'Make less noise or I'll fettle your canister for you.' In the dialect of the time, it was an expressive way to threaten extreme injury.

Other constables were called, but none could trace the place where this was coming from, and after some time, more shouts were heard. This time, Bower heard a call of 'Mr Smith!' and 'Police!' Looking up, he saw the figure of a woman walking on a high roof. Bower saw Liz roll from the high roof to a lower one, then scramble a little before she lost her grip and fell down to her death.

The medical examination was done by Dr Leason, and he testified in court that Liz had several bruises which had been

caused by being beaten by fists. It became clear, when the room and landing where the group had been were examined, that the woman had been attacked, then struggled, and broken free. There were bloodstains on walls and on the stairs. Statements made about the medical examinations revealed a sad and desperate life Liz was

The Queen's Hotel. The author

leading. She had a few pence stitched into her stocking, and a witness had said that when the deceased had left her lodgings on the morning of the day she died, she had only a penny on her.

Liz had been with Gray when the argument began, and it had been a sordid and nasty row over the cost of her services: a familiar scenario in the lives of these unfortunate women. She had broken away and taken the only exit to freedom that seemed open to her. The point in court was whether or not Gray was guilty of wilful murder? The jury found that he was. He was destined for the next assizes and a death sentence.

It was a heavy day for the women of Liz Shepherd's trade: as if this horrendous assault was not enough, there was a suicide at the same time, a poor woman had hanged herself. It had only taken fifteen inches of rope fixed on a bedroom cornice to end the life of poor Rebecca Burgin. The coroner's inquest, held at the *Northumberland Arms*, was assured that there was no other factor in the death: it was an uncomplicated self-murder.

These cases highlight the perilous lives of the oldest profession, and Bradford had had its share of these women for some time: at the very same time as this murder, William Logan was writing his book, *The Great Social Evil*, and he noted about Bradford:

> *The Chief Constable for Bradford, in his report of 1851, that the number of known brothels within the borough was forty-two; the number of known prostitutes residing in them was 109; the number of these residing in thirteen beerhouses in the borough, twenty-one – total 130.*

Almost every week in the press reports throughout the nineteenth century, there was some woman being attacked while in the course of her professional work. In Liz Shepherd's case, she did not even have a 'minder' and worked alone.

CHAPTER 19

A Shooting and a Bad Hanging
1876–77

. . . his death was slow and horrific.

This is a story of an argument that got well out of hand, and of the calamitous results of this: a tale of a row in a public house leading to an agonising death and a very quick death.

It started on Boxing Day, 1876 when thirty-seven-year-old John Johnson was enjoying a drink with Amelia Walker in the saloon of the *Bedford Arms* in Wakefield Road. Everything was convivial; they were enjoying each other's company and the mood was relaxed. But Amelia had enjoyed quite a number of men's company in her short life (she was only twenty-four), and as she went out the back to go to the toilet outside, she met one of her former associates, a certain Amos White. In the reports, he is called simply, 'an old friend' but there is a deep rancour in their relationship, and it figures prominently here.

White put a hand on her and was becoming a little too friendly, so Amelia called for help, and of course, Johnson came running from the bar to help her. The men began to fight. White was going to get the better of his opponent, and Johnson was not going to lose in this encounter. He ran off, only to return with a gun.

Johnson wasted no time in finding his victim, going

The Bedford Arms. Laura Carter

directly to him and firing the shotgun into his chest. White did not take long to die; bystanders grabbed the killer and wrestled him to the ground. It was no problem having him taken into custody. This was all a plain, uncomplicated narrative to a man who had taken one beer too many going to extremes to settle a score. The whole affair becomes messy when it comes to the time when Johnson was called to meet his Maker for the crime, as indeed he was: the death sentence was the only option in these circumstances, of course.

Johnson, in York Castle, had the misfortune to be a client of one of the most inept hangmen in the chronicles of that profession. This was Thomas Askern. Along with the inconsistent later executioner, William Calcraft, Askern was not one who inspired confidence in the people around him when it came to the fatal appointment of killer with his dying moments on the scaffold. Johnson was in for a rough time.

Askern was always hard up, always in debt, and on this occasion, notably inadequate to do the job with any care or sensitivity. When Johnson was made ready for the last seconds, standing on the trap, on 3 April 1877, the lever was pulled but the trap broke and Johnson fell through the hole, his feet not kicking air but still on wood. He had to be sat down and attended by the warders of the gaol, who were always ready to help a poor criminal if the death was being too slow and agonising. At that time, the knot was usually tied so that the neck muscles and bone would be wrenched broken, and so death could take some time. Warders might have to pull on dangling legs sometimes.

But on this occasion, Johnson had to be taken to the trapdoor and prepared again. The man's heart must have been bursting from his chest, and whatever resolve he had gathered was surely gone, as he was trying to prepare for death a second time. It was a total outrage: the drop was only partly successful and his death was slow and horrific. He struggled for several minutes in his death throes.

It is outrageous that Askern was still doing this work for a few years after this, until William Marwood of Horncastle developed the 'long drop' which made death much cleaner and quicker. Ironically, Marwood had already began using this method, in practice, when Askern was in business, as a provincial hangman, rather than the official national hangman. This post was to come with the arrival of Marwood and of Bradford executioner, James Berry.

It was not as if Askern had not had experience: he had been drawn from the inmate population when he first began, then famously hanged the notorious Mary Ann Cotton in Durham three years earlier, and also executed a teenager in Dumfries in what was the last public hanging in Scotland.

None of this would have been of any comfort to the hapless killer, John Johnson.

James Berry, the Bradford executioner. Laura Carter

CHAPTER 20

A Deadly Rage Against a Neighbour
1878

I'll cut thy throat an'all.

Anthony Owston, a man possessed utterly by jealousy, rushed into the shop next door to his home and confronted the grocer, John Smith, with the words, 'I will cut thy throat an'all and then my own!' Owston set about the deadly business with a will, and thrashed around, smashing everything in his way, cutting first the air and then the grocer's arms with a long blade. If it had not been for a shop assistant bravely throwing himself as a protective cushion between them there would have been a second murder.

That little phrase, 'I'll cut thy throat an'all' referred to the fact that on the floor of his own house, his wife Jane was lying dead in a pool of blood, her throat cut so deeply that her windpipe was severed completely. The man had killed the woman he loved most in the world in a crazed fit of jealous passion, and this family of the two adults and four children, was to be ruined forever on this October day.

It had all begun with Jane's alcoholism: she had gradually become a drunk, and neglected everything in her life for the sake of the next bottle. The fact that John Smith, the grocer next door, also had a beer-shop was temptation too hard to resist and she started spending most of her day there, leaving the children and the housekeeping to whatever might happen.

Jane had reached the point of desperation: she had sold or pawned everything she could, and had even started inventing stories to borrow goods from neighbours to pawn or sell, making feeble or outlandish excuses when things went wrong. It is clear that the Owstons were held in very low regard around

The Owston Murder. Laura Carter, from an old illustration. Police Gazette

the Westgrove Street area (off Sunbridge Road). Owston was more and more certain that his wife was spending time at the shop with Smith just to do anything to have more alcohol. In his mind, this was a dark thought that led to the most twisted and unhealthy reflections on what might be happening while he was away at work.

Things were bound to come to a head, and they did when, just a week before the murderous attack, his suspicions had led him to think that his wife and Smith were planning to run away together. The grocer's wife had already left him, and it was looking as though an affair with Jane Owston was the cause. It was all too much to bear. At that point, full of a violent passion, he had grabbed hold of his wife and said, 'Hold on there!' then he had assaulted Smith.

His plan was to kill his wife first, then Smith, and finally himself. He virtually succeeded, as, when the attempt to kill Smith was thwarted, he slashed into his own throat with the knife. The events after that were dramatic in the extreme. He staggered home, blood streaming from him and gasping for breath, to find that the police had arrived and were standing by the corpse of his wife. Poor Owston broke down, and confessed, then begged to be allowed to write something down. There was this man, still in a terrible rage, blood dripping onto the paper as he wrote, expressing his dreadful act in this way:

I believed they were both going to run away at once. I am guilty and I hope she is dead, and may God forgive me, and I hope my children will be good boys and girls. I have tried to guard against . . . . But she has been determined leave me. Let me die. [The missing word will never be known, as a drop of blood erased it.]

Owston was bandaged in court four months later. The main development, expressed now that there was some semblance of a return to sanity, or at least a cold look at those awful events, was that Jane had refused to sleep with her husband. He said, plaintively, 'I cannot give up Jane. I loved her as a boy and I loved her as a man.' If he could not have her, no-one else could. It became clear that these actions were those of a man without a sane mental condition, in spite of a planned intention to kill. He was sent to a lunatic asylum, and we are bound to think, knowing that he had a sister already in that place, that there was in truth some profound mental disease affecting Owston. The complete emotional wreck that first met the gaze of the police officers was likely to have been a decisive factor.

We are bound to feel some concern about Owston's fate, most likely that of being placed in York Lunatic Asylum. In the early years of the nineteenth century, it had been subject to corruption and mismanagement; in 1813 the governor was sacked and in 1820 the apothecary was also dismissed, this time for sexual relations with an inmate. Hopefully, there was a more humane regime by this date, but Owston's destiny was going to be miserable in the extreme.

CHAPTER 21

The Ripper in Bradford?
1888

... there had been extreme
mutilation of the body ...

This murder case has been dealt with in my *Unsolved Yorkshire Murders* (2004) but there is a little up-dating to add, so first, here are the salient points of this story. It has been suggested, with some confidence, that Jack the Ripper came to Bradford in this year, and murdered a young boy. It was a most brutal killing, and with all the trappings and hallmarks of Jack himself, a long way from his patch.

Just after Christmas 1888, John Gill, of Thorncliff Road, went for a ride on a milkcart. It was very early in the morning, and his mother never saw him alive again. He had been seen playing but also, menacingly, he was seen talking to a man, a stranger to the area by all accounts. The family soon felt the distress of his absence, and feared the worst; they placed a poster on view, with a physical description of him, and actually used the word 'lost' despite the fact that it was only one day after his disappearance.

John, eight years old, was found in a stable by Joe Buckle, a butcher. Joe was cleaning the place when he saw a pile of some indescribable object, and looking closer, he saw that it was a corpse, and most noticeable on first inspection was the detail that one ear had been cut off. He ran for help. When closer inspection took place, by officers, it was found that there had been extreme mutilation of the boy; his stomach had been cut open and vital organs placed on him. He had been repeatedly cut, stabbed in the chest, and there was a rough noose around his neck.

This is where the complex business of the massive number of Ripper letters figures in the story. The pathology certainly

Dear Boss,

I keep on hearing the police have caught me but they won't fix Me just yet. I have laughed when they look so clever and talk about being on the right track. That joke about leather apron gave me real fits. I am down on whores and I shan't quit ripping them till I do get buckled. Grand work the last job was. I gave the lady no time to squeal. How can they catch me now. I love my work and want to start again. You will soon hear of me with my funny little games. I saved some of the proper red stuff in a ginger beer bottle over the last job to write with but it went thick like glue...

One of the original Ripper letters. Author's collection

makes the Gill murder a contender for being classified as a Ripper killing; Dr Bond, writing about Mary Kelly's body, noted that 'the viscera were found in various parts . . . the liver between the feet and the spleen by the left side of the body.' There are similarities, but the main argument for the Ripper coming north rests on statements made in the letters. As Philip Sugden has written, 'The important question is . . . whether any of these letters we have noticed was written by the murderer.' This was said about the first letters received, well before the Bradford case. By the time of the Gill case, police were walking into Whitechapel in pairs; five killings had taken place, the last in November, just a month before the Bradford death.

At the end of November, one of the Ripper letters had the text, 'I shall do another murder on some young youth such as printing lads who work in the city. I did write you once before . . . I shall do them worse than the women, I shall take their hearts . . . .' But the problem with Patricia Cornwell's use of the Ripper letters in associating the Bradford case with Jack is that she talks of the 'Ripper letters' as if it is certain that there was one author (see her *Portrait of a Killer*). This is why she dismisses the most tantalising scrap of detail in poor John Gill's murder: that a piece of a Liverpool newspaper was used to wrap part of the body. Even more fascinating, the paper had a name on it: 'W. Mason, Derby Road'.

Those ripperologists who think that the man was James Maybrick, merchant, of Liverpool, would perhaps point to the fact that Maybrick was most probably meeting someone in Manchester at one point in the year 1888, but otherwise, apparently never went near Bradford. Recent writing on Maybrick, and notably the new work done by experts on *The Ripper Diary* would seem to confirm that there is no factual reference to a Bradford connection. We have known for a long time that there was a Lancashire connection, because of James Bierley, from Rochdale, who was linked to the Maybrick family.

Naturally, the Ripper letters in the hand that Cornwell believes was that of the painter, Walter Sickert, also contain one text which reads, 'I riped [*sic*] up a little boy in Bradford' and another one has the date, 'January 16, Bradford'. The great Sherlock Holmes would have reacted to this by insisting that, though these Bradford letters may have been by the same hand, there is nothing to prove that they belonged to the man we know as Jack the Ripper. In other words, what we most likely have here is that well-known phenomenon in homicide, the copycat crime.

As far as the Bradford connection is concerned, the events could have turned out tragically for the prime suspect in the city, one Bill Barrett, the dairyman, but he was cleared and had had 'a long interview with his legal adviser' that was undoubtedly a basis for a sound defence. The only evidence was circumstantial. If the killing was a copycat murder, then the identity of the real killer remains a mystery, and the Gill case is in the annals of unsolved cases.

The Bradford case is not the only one that may be another Ripper victim. In June 1887, at Temple Stairs on the Thames, parts of a body previously found at Rainham were discovered in a parcel. At the inquest it was asserted that someone with a knowledge of anatomy had done this ghastly murder. Eventually, as in the Bradford scenario, a letter supposedly from the 'real' Ripper denied any involvement with these body parts. At least the Bradford killing had some definite pointers to the real Ripper.

CHAPTER 22

Violence at the Manningham Strike 1891

... the Durham Light Infantry charged the crowd.

On April, 1891, the Mayor of Bradford read out the Riot Act by the light of a lantern. His streets were very dark and the mood was sombre. As he read, stones were thrown at him and two of these hit him on the chest.

This was all a response to a strike at Manningham Mills, and there was some kind of hex on the place: it had been burned down in 1873 and then rebuilt. The new eleven acre building was undoubtedly fine and impressive, employing 400 people and enjoying the fame of being the most complete mill in Europe. But this strike was severe, lasting nineteen weeks from December 1890 to April 1891. The riot was the culmination of this.

Lister's Mill. Laura Carter

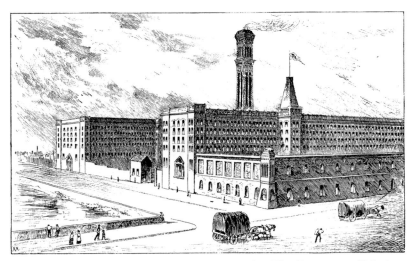

Manningham Mills, illustration from James Burnley, The Romance of Modern Industry, *1880.* Author's collection

In everyday speech, parents might talk casually of 'reading the riot act' if there is a family row but in fact, at the heart of the text of the real thing, we have something that, when read publicly before the sovereign's subjects, is a fearful statement:

> *Our Sovereign Lord the King chargeth and commandeth all persons here assembled immediately to disperse themselves, and peaceable to depart to their habitations or to their lawful business on pain of death.*
> GOD SAVE THE QUEEN

Although it is hard to believe, almost 3,000 people had gathered for an illegal meeting, a spin-off from the speeches made by leading radicals to the workers concerned in the Manningham strike, and perhaps even more stunning, after a period of unrest and violence, the Durham Light Infantry charged the crowd.

This was a Sunday afternoon, and the Bradford police had made a statement banning a meeting. But there was a famous trade union leader and speaker present: Ben Tillett. Ordinary working folk would have desperately wanted to hear him. Councillor Sanders, from Rotherham, was also involved in planning this meeting, along with William Byles, and trouble

Ben Tillett, union leader. Laura Carter

was expected. The police had a staunch leader in their Chief Officer, James Withers. He was an experienced man, and had controlled Bradford for sixteen years before this. It must have been one of his stiffest tasks. He had 150 officers ready and stationed in the Town Hall when the crowd gathered. Their first objective was to arrest Sanders, and they succeeded in this, but agreed to release him if he swore not to act the demagogue and rouse the people to action.

The situation simmered through to Monday, and a crowd was still gathered, expectant and ready for a confrontation. Police stayed in place in the afternoon and, by the evening, people began throwing stones at them; charges by police led to arrests, but it was going to be too much for them. The soldiers arrived at nine in the evening. It was at this juncture that the Riot Act was read to them, and Major Woodland led a force to crush the rioters. It was a terrible sight for ordinary people to see: the police had truncheons, but the troops had bayonets fixed. It was going to be Peterloo over again, many thought. At that similar meeting in Manchester, eleven people were killed and over 400 were injured as the hussars charged.

The Bradford crowd was dispersed, and fragmented, with knots of men pushed into adjoining streets. Order was restored by eleven that night, and there were two very severely wounded people who had been struck by the officers, and were now carried off for treatment in the Town Hall.

Ben Tillett, the main guest speaker, must have been alarmed and amazed at these events. But confrontation was nothing new to him, as he had helped in the fight for the 'Dockers' Tanner' in 1889. Tillett was to go on to play a large part in the formation of the Transport and General Workers' Union in 1922, but his day in Bradford must have been one of his toughest experiences. The fact is that, as we read the account of these troubles today, the disappearance of Tillett from the scene is most noticeable, and in his memoirs, written many years later, he makes no mention of this incident. He became a major figure in Labour history and his years were crowded with more significant events.

One possibility is that Bradford had gained something of a reputation for militancy. After all, the city's track record in terms of the active radicalism there, from the Chartists through to open antagonisms centred in labour strife, was not impressive if we see that history through the eyes of a Chief Constable.

Many must have thought that the protest was played out. Not so. The crowd came yet again the next day. Rioting began in earnest when darkness fell; this time there was a deep grievance at what the authorities had done; thousands were pressed near the Town hall and police, soldiers and special constables gathered to act once again. They had to act quickly, because there was a more evident sense of menace now. Property was being smashed at random; some of the Town Hall windows had been broken. It became a case of treating this as a holding operation, limiting the area in which the rioters could act. Gradually, it faded, and the restraint helped the situation, despite the threatening phrase in the Riot Act of 'on pain of death'. The newspaper report at the time claimed that there had been damage done to the cost of £500 for the windows alone. As with most major public disturbances in Victorian cities, this Bradford confrontation was dealt with by both discretion and force. Good politics and common sense prevented another Peterloo.

CHAPTER 23

No Reprieve:
The Ellwood Case
1908

... another client of executioner Henry Pierrepoint ...

On a summer's day in 1908, the city of Bradford was shocked by the breaking news of a brutal murder, and it was most disturbing as it happened in the afternoon. Thomas Wilkinson, working at Fieldhouse and Jowett in Swain Street, was beaten to death by someone wielding a poker, and the killer had brought the weapon with him, as there was no coal fire in the store.

The murderer was not exactly careful to cover his tracks or to hide his identity in any way; not only had he been seen standing in the doorway by a passer-by, looking troubled, and actually saying that 'They were having a bit of bother in the office,' but he also bought the poker just down the road, as Samuel Ellis, who sold him the weapon, was to testify.

From these details, it would appear that there may not have been a motive, as it was the nasty work of someone who was distracted in the extreme, but there was in fact a clear motive. The killer was John Ellwood, and he had worked for Fieldhouse and Jowett, leaving that employment about six months before this incident. He had been involved in a heated row with his employers and had left under a cloud; it was therefore not hard for the police to show that, as an employee, he would know the routine of the place in a typical week, and would therefore be aware that large amounts of money were brought to the building by the company cashier every Friday. It was no coincidence, perhaps, that Ellwood had arranged to visit the premises at two o'clock that afternoon, Friday 31 July. There had been correspondence, and both Ellwood and Wilkinson had written or rung up to leave messages. There was also the testimony of the landlord of the Fountain Brewery, who had seen the accused leave his pub just before the time of the killing.

It was hardly going to be a problem for the investigating officers, as there was plenty of blood on Ellwood's clothes when he was arrested, and his pathetic excuse that the cause of this was merely a bleeding nose was not going to fool anyone. His line of thought regarding his reasons for being seen at the murder scene that day by the man going by (he was Isaac Pollard) was simply that Wilkinson was trying to have him reinstated in his post; Mrs Ellwood produced evidence of a letter from Wilkinson to that effect, and also stated that her husband had been with her at home at the time of the murder.

All fairly straightforward, we might think. When he appeared at Leeds Assizes on 12 November that year, and it was discussed that Ellwood's intention was to have a wages cheque, intended for the employees of the mills, to be cashed. Ellwood, it was claimed, was planning to rob Wilkinson of that cash. Later, at appeal, it was stated that a witness who had been bound over to attend the trial had not actually been called, and the lawyers at the time argued that this evidence would not have been helpful for the defence case.

At the Court of Appeal on 20 November, Mr Gregory Ellis, for the applicant Ellwood, argued that at the trial there was no motive for the murder defined and explained. The supposed letter from Wilkinson inviting him to come regarding a job had been dismissed, but Ellwood's defence brought this up again. Mr Justice Channel explained the situation, as Ellwood stood and wondered if he was to be saved from the noose, that, '... there is a great deal of difference between absence of proved motive and proved absence of motive.' In other words, that the accused planned to go to the premises and steal, and to steal even at the cost of a life, appeared to be the motive, and no letter arranging a meeting would cast doubt on that. After all, he had been seen by a man at the time, and it was known that he had bought the poker. There was no ambiguity in the material evidence of the nature of the killing: the victim was battered brutally and relentlessly, the wounds inflicted by the poker.

The appeal was refused. John Ellwood became another client of executioner Henry Pierrepoint, and he was hanged on 3 December 1908 at Armley Gaol.

CHAPTER 24

The Carving Knife Killing 1910

There was a bloodstained carving knife near to his body.

Even a cursory look at the murder cases in Edwardian times soon leads one to the conclusion that there were an astoundingly high number of suicides and also of domestic assaults in that period. Research has shown that for both these crimes, there was a marked increase of incidences between the 1870s and c.1910. It is not difficult to find reasons: there was a massive new commuter class working long hours, and also long hours in shops, factories and mills took their toll on people's self-control.

An even more obvious place to look for the triggers that fused violence between partners was in the very high number of beer-shops and pubs at this time. Working people in mills and factories would often drink a few pints of beer in the morning, before the working day. Drink was surely the main catalyst in tragic stories of husbands killing wives, and this was so with John Coulson, a man who had the indignity of having a summons served him while he was at work, and it was based on a charge of assault on his wife, Jane.

The neighbourhood knew that there were problems with the Coulsons. There had been frequent rows before the events of 24 May 1910, when John went to pawn his wife's wedding ring and a neighbour, calling at the Coulson home very early, had no reply from the woman of the house. But the man's recklessness knew no bounds: the summons at work had a statement written on the back that John Coulson had killed his wife and son. In the pub that evening, the summons and the awful note were passed around once again. It comes as a surprise to learn that

ODD-HANDED JUSTICE.—*First Ruffian.* "Wot was I hup for, and wot 'ave I got ?
Well, I floor'd a woman and took 'er watch, and I've got two years and a floggin'."
Second Ruffian. "Ha !—*I* flung a woman out o' the top floor winder; an' I've on'y got
three months !" *First Ruffian.* "Ah, but then *she was yer wife ! !*"

Cartoon on violence to wives. Punch

two police constables, after this story was circulated and people
spoke to the law, called at Coulson's house in Springfield Place,
Dudley Hill, and made enquiries, yet went away without more
than a chat taking place.

But Constable Walker returned late that night, still troubled
by the story, and he knew that there had been a long history of
aggressive and violent behaviour between the couple. He forced
entry this time, and when he walked through into the bedroom,
he saw two bodies: on the floor there was Jane Coulson, and her
five-year-old son, Thomas, lying on the bed. There was a bloodstained carving knife near to his body.

As with so many domestic murders of this kind (the Owston
story for instance) there is an element of farce or black humour,
and this is no exception, because John arrived home later,
absolutely drenched. His story was that he had tried to kill
himself, in a fit of black despair, but had failed. Trying to
picture that scene forces a conclusion of either the sad tale of a

man at the end of his tether, or a violent and selfish man still in a violent passion, and still intent on preserving himself, with no profound remorse. Coulson was arrested and charged with two murders.

There have been some very speedy trials over the years, such as a famously quick trial in Lincoln in which the jury took only six minutes to reach a guilty decision, but this case presents a possible record in this regard: the jury did not even leave their box; they simply expressed a unanimous and assured verdict of guilty, and John Coulson gave Pierrepoint yet more work. Coulson was only thirty-two when he was hanged in Leeds on 9 August that year.

CHAPTER 25

Battered to Death
1924

... someone arrived to bludgeon her with a coal-hammer ...

When *The Times* first published a rather hurried and inaccurate report of a nasty murder in a Bradford terraced house, they found most interest in the fact that there was a large amount of paper money on the premises, and they had been told that 'some £10 Bank of England notes may be missing.' Little did they know that this detail would turn out to be the decisive factor in tracking down a murderer.

Sixty-year-old widow Elizabeth Reaney (formerly Hudson) thought that she was about to move from Sunderland Road, Manningham, to a new life in Derby when she was seen at her door, looking around, in February 1924. Neighbours said she seemed as though she was waiting for someone. She did have an appointment with someone, but that person turned out to be her killer, and that day when she was looking down the street was the last day she was seen alive.

She had been taking money from her account from the time she had arranged to give the buyer vacant possession, and there was plenty of cash in the house when someone arrived to bludgeon her with a coal-hammer on 22 February. She had been severely mutilated in a frenzied and brutal attack when her body was found on the afternoon of the day after her murder. There were no immediate suspects, but police found four letters in the house, with the signature of a Mr Goodson, and posted from Leeds. When attempts were made to trace this man and the address, it was found that there was no such person. Suspicions were aroused.

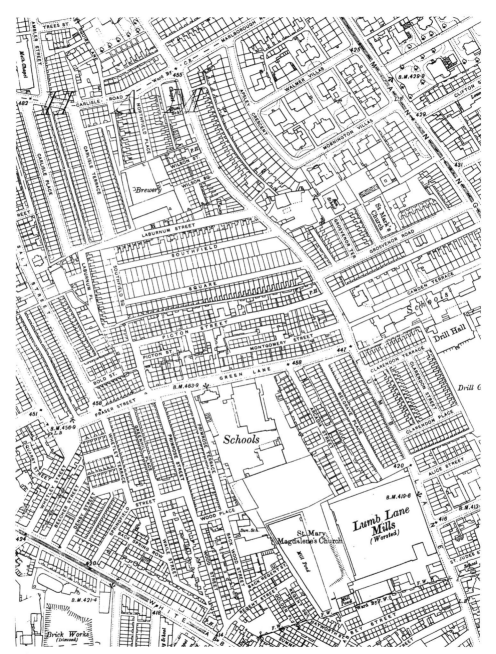

The crowded streets around Manningham and Sunderland Road. Ordnance Survey, 1906

The Murder House, Sunderland Road. Laura Carter

Good police work and sheer persistence led to the discovery of a name linked to the letters and to the deal involving the house: it turned out that Elizabeth had been fooled. There was no buyer, just a man of questionable character called William Wardell. Detectives traced the man to his haunts and interest centred on the Peel Hotel where he did most of his drinking. Interviews led to the discovery that he had left that pub at around quarter past ten on the night of the murder, and there was a witness called Leonard Heseltine, who had been with Wardell that evening and had walked with him to Longside Lane, close to what is now the University of Bradford. Usually on occasions like this, Wardell would be going to a fish and chip shop. But Sunderland Road was not much further, on the corner with Oak Lane.

It was surely a difficult time for Heseltine when he found himself again in Wardell's company at the *Peel Hotel*, because he talked about what had happened during the police enquiries, and he suggested that the best course of action was to go and clear his name with the law. The man was undoubtedly unskilled in thinking ahead and in doing the obvious things to avoid suspicion, because when he took his friend's advice and was subsequently searched and interviewed, bank notes were found on him whose numbers matched the notes found in the house of the murdered woman. Here was a man of forty-seven who had tricked a vulnerable widow into parting with money, and into the belief that she had a home waiting for her elsewhere; and he had eventually come to her own home and slaughtered her there.

It was with a mounting sense of having 'got their man' that police put Wardell's signature next to the name at the foot of the letters sent to Mrs Reaney and found a good match. Almost as if he were so clumsy that he wanted to be found and linked to the crime, he also had a notebook on him with the words, 'Goodson ... Leeds', recorded in it.

Apart from the notes and the letters, there was never any blood found on his garments, but Wardell tried to tell a story about how he came by the notes; it was unsuccessful, as he was found guilty of wilful murder. He was hanged at Armley on 18 June that year.

CHAPTER 26

The Moneylender Meets his End
1931

There was a certain dark fate at play ...

A young man went to spray some money around one July day in 1930; he paid some rent, and then he bought railway tickets, and even gave his girl some spending money. Then they went into a bar and bought drinks – for anyone who happened to be there. The man was only a mill worker, not someone you might expect to have a roll in his pocket and a carefree way with cash. There had to be a story behind this, and indeed there was. It was a sad and terrible one.

Young Fred Gill, an electric motor driver from Keighley, had problems, and they were all about money – or the lack of it. It was a time of economic depression; the Wall Street Crash of 1929 and its reverberations across Europe contributed to the decline in the textile trades at this time, and Fred, along with his girlfriend Nellie Rickerby, were two of many thousands of victims. But Fred's solution was not a wise one, and it involved being deeply into the troubles caused by mounting debts.

Fred had been planning a holiday in Whitehaven with Nellie, and she had been bringing cash to him for that purpose, with him acting as treasurer; but he was not exactly trustworthy. Nellie worked in a very tough job, at Bairstow's, as a twister; this was a worsted mill and her work meant the hard labour of repairing snapped threads in the spinning shop, with lots of noise over the long shift. If anyone deserved a holiday, it was Nellie.

Fred had also been working in the textile industry, for Prince Smith, but his work had been reduced to short time as orders

Keighley at the time of the murder. Laura Carter

declined. He was becoming one of the many poor folk around the streets at that dark time. He spent the holiday money and had only one option: to borrow from a moneylender. In fact, he had a long-standing debt, owed to Oliver Preston, who had his office at Bradford Road, Keighley, but lived in Oakworth. Preston was intent on piling on the pressure as far as Gill was concerned. The daunting solicitor's letter was sent out. Fred Gill wrote to several other moneylenders, trying to borrow other sums of money in order to pay this main debt off.

Preston was a family man and a member of the Liberal Club. He was a successful and generally familiar and notable figure in the business life of the area. His letter had forced his debtor into a momentous and very bold decision: his only option in fact. This was to rob his tormentor. The stress on him was so much that it was coming to the point at which he would have to tell Nellie that he had spent the holiday money. The shame was clearly too much to bear or even to contemplate.

Oliver Preston's House in Oakworth. Laura Cart

Fred Gill was working at the blacksmith's workshop at Prince

The street where the killer lived (now demolished). Laura Carter

Smith and there, in front of him, was a pile of metal bars suitable to use as pokers, and indeed a colleague saw Fred sorting through these, and recalled hearing him say he was looking for a poker. He had thought out the attack he was to make on Preston; this involved hanging around the Station Buildings, close to Preston's office, and maybe going for a haircut – he was careful to tell people this. There was a certain dark fate at play in this case as far as the moneylender was concerned, because he was planning to leave for a lone holiday in Scotland after that day's work, and he had a suitcase with him when he left home.

Attacks on businessmen who had cash on the premises have always been common: 'bookies' are often targets; but borrowing money is something with a moral stigma attached, and it was unusual that Gill was not very discreet about his dealings with Preston. People had known that he was trying to borrow money, and even more fateful for the killer, people had seen him enter Preston's office on the night of the killing. He never tried to skulk around and creep in unobserved, for the sake of any reputation he might have. So clumsy and rough was the attack that there was even a witness – at least a person who heard things happening at the other side of the locked door. This was an Oakworth nightwatchman: he actually heard 'something like a groan or a grunt' and also he heard someone struggling to lock the door from the inside.

The dying moneylender was discovered by a barber the next morning. He saw Preston on the couch, covered in blood. There had been a struggle and part of the room was wrecked. Amazingly, the metal rod was left on the floor. There was no problem for the police when it came to sorting out a motive: a roll of notes had been taken from the dead man's pocket; the elastic band was there and the inner pocket pulled out for all to see. Preston was not yet dead: he was brought out on a stretcher and he had a cloth over his face, but witnesses saw that he was moving at that time. It was going to be a long and futile effort to try to save his life in the Victoria Hospital in Keighley that day. He died two days after the attack, his skull fractured.

The arrest was quick and assured. There was to be no complexity in the Preston case. He was committed to Leeds Assizes. Gill's only explanations for the cash and for the possession of the iron bar were pathetically weak, claiming he had won money at the races, and that, despite witness statements, he had never been near the pile of bars at the works.

There was a notably determined effort on the part of the defence lawyer to try to avert the death penalty, including a petition signed by 19,000 people. But Gill was hanged at Armley on 4 February the following year. There was no question of any extenuating circumstances relating to his stressful situation and need to take desperate action. In the 1930s, there had been sentences of death by the dozen on men who had done similarly rash and senseless acts under pressure of either money problems or emotional entanglements. Why should this man be any exception? That was the mood at the time, although many would say that great market forces and world economic processes had their part in this sorry tale.

CHAPTER 27

Murder at the Piggery 1932

Gill had been severely battered . . .

When fifty-five-year-old Alfred Gill was found dead at Tyersal, Pudsey, in December 1931, his watch had stopped. The time frozen, most likely at the point of death, was 6.13. It was a terrible shock for his two sons, who had the ill luck to be the ones who found him, after an increasingly worrying gap of time passing since he left home the previous day. Gill had been severely battered and was in a horrific state when found.

Gill was a businessman, mostly working as a greengrocer at his premises in Leeds Road, Bradford. But he had other concerns, such as a mobile branch to his retail outlet. He seems to have worked hard and mostly alone, but he did have occasional help from John Roberts, a young man who put in some hours either in the shops or in the piggeries, another subsidiary business Gill had going. Mrs Gill did not see much of her husband: he was ambitious and very industrious, and his time at home was not much at all, so when his wife Louisa saw him leave for work at nine in the morning of 11 December, she might have expected him to be late home, but she was destined to have a shock and a great deal of worry coming her way.

The grocer was not home by eight that night, so Louisa and their two sons went out to search for Alfred. People had said that they had seen him at various points through the day: he had been seen with Roberts at mid-afternoon. A witness called Betts saw him at the piggeries opening a gate. But there must have been some worry, particularly as he had been carrying a considerable amount of cash – £50 in fact, and with more to be

gathered as the day went on. All the usual haunts were visited –
even the piggeries, but no sign of the man was found.

It was not until early afternoon the next day that the two sons,
Alfred and William, went again to the piggeries and that the body
was found. As with the Keighley case of the murder of Preston,
there was to be a similar motive here: young Roberts was
strapped for cash. When questions began to be asked, there was
only one name on people's lips: no known enemies, no business
rivalry, but a young part-timer who was always hard up. That is
what it proved to be; Roberts had been a debtor and had been in
court to settle a debt, a weekly payment placed on him. When
investigations went further, there were to be other clear leads.

Most patently suspicious was the fact that he was seen with
one of his employer's horses, and also a few people noticed that
Roberts had a black eye. When good solid police work traced the
man's lifestyle through his leisure habits, they were led to a pub,
the *Ring o' Bells*, and statements were made that would condemn the man: mainly that he was noticed to have left the pub
to change his clothes. With hindsight, it appears thoughtless in
the extreme for a man in his position not to have destroyed the
clothes he had worn when he attacked Gill. They were bloodstained, and the police retrieved them. Roberts was doomed.

The accused could only say, in explanation, that there had
been a row at the piggeries and that Gill had provoked him. The
detail that Roberts, stung into action by insults, landed a punch
on his boss, but there just happened to be a hammer lying
nearby, and Roberts claimed that Gill had tried to strike him
with that.

The provocation and self-defence case was flimsy; the fact was
that Roberts had struck Gill with a brick; the grocer had been
repeatedly battered: one blow given in anger might have caused
a cut and left Gill with a nasty headache, but he would have
walked out of the place. Such was the reasoning at the appeal for
the case: there is a huge difference between a 'glancing blow'
and a vicious attack in a frenzy. Mister Justice Humpreys was
the judge, and he and the jury had no problem with the very
straightforward prosecution work done by Walter Hedley.

John Henry Roberts was hanged in Leeds by Thomas
Pierrepoint on 28 April 1932.

Chapter 28

Petit Mal was no Defence
1934

She fell backwards and her life ebbed away.

When Louis Hamilton bundled his wife into her mother's house in Jermyn Street, Stott Hill, on Boxing Day, 1933, he was possessed by a blind rage. It was a passion he had known before, and it had been directed at his new wife, Maud, who was only twenty-three and had given birth to their son not long before this. Louis forced her inside, and it was noisy; there was nothing discreet about his actions, and there never had been. He was fond of yelling out threats that he would kick doors in if he didn't get what he wanted.

He had been in trouble, not long before, for assault after kicking her and swearing at her. A summons had been given to him and he was roused to anger by this. His moods normally led to this kind of scene, and nothing more.

This time, though, instead of a slap or a punch, as he had done in the past, Louis had a knife. He fumed and screamed at Maud, and slashed her across the throat with the blade. He caught her this way as she was standing up from a chair. The door had been bolted behind them and he was in control. She fell backwards and her life ebbed away.

Their life had been very difficult; they had known each other for many years, and had married eventually in July 1933. Maud was pregnant when they wed, and the couple, as happened so often at that time, moved in to live with Hamilton's sister Beatrice. Louis and Maud tried to exist separate from the child, who was, in effect, 'in care' with Beatrice. But this never would have worked out well. Maud went back to her parents. Louis was left to smoulder with resentment in the background, his hatred building up every day until it reached intolerable proportions and he was gripped with a violent rage. He spent time with his brother-in-law, a man who had the misfortune to have to listen to the brooding anger of this sick man.

Maud had been visiting neighbours that Boxing Day when Louis struck. His murderous attack was to be in public, with a crowd gathering outside. When the killer did emerge from the house, there was a constable waiting for him. This was to prove a crucially important event, because Hamilton, as a crowd took him to the officer, said, 'I quite realise what I have done.' When asked about this in court, the officer added that the accused seemed to be 'dazed' when arrested. This raised the whole issue of Hamilton's epilepsy.

The defence argued that Hamilton was suffering from a *petit mal* attack when he went into the rage. This is the less severe form of epileptic attack, compared with the more enervating *grand mal* episode suffered by epileptics. The statement made to the police and the observations of the officer on the spot were all that the defence could call on with any substance. Although Hamilton's father had suffered from epilepsy, it was always going to be difficult to make a case here, bearing in mind that the many previous violent attacks had been made with intent, and always directed at the one person: Maud. The only slight factor involved in the consideration of the crime in this instance led to the jury recommending mercy. That could potentially make the sentence life imprisonment with hard labour. There was no linked medical treatment or special circumstances of the sentence conditions.

Several murder cases in the 1930s hinged on the rather limited knowledge of mental illness at that time, and some were more complex than this case. It seems inevitable that the verdict would be wilful murder, with no extenuating circumstances, and so it was. Hamilton was yet another customer for Thomas Pierrepoint and his noose.

CHAPTER 29

A Child-Murder Mystery 1938

Phyllis had been savagely attacked . . .

In July, 1969, the *Yorkshire Post* writer Frank Laws wrote a feature on the unsolved murder of eight-year-old Phyllis Hirst forty years earlier. A boxed announcement in the feature stated that the case was still open: 'The police file on this case remains open. Anyone with additional evidence which might lead to an arrest should contact the nearest police station . . . .' It has always proved to be a mystery, and the truth of how and why the girl was killed in a lane near All Saints' Church, Little Horton Green, recedes further with every passing day.

This case has been covered in my *Unsolved Yorkshire Murders* (2004), but there are some details that were not included in that story, so I add them here. First, the bare facts: Phyllis was the daughter of a painter who lived in Sterling Street, and had

been out playing, as normal, in the area around her house, on an evening late in October. Her body was found that evening in the lane, but forensic evidence showed that she had not been killed on that spot. There was brickdust found in her fingernails suggested that she died near building works. The girl had been seen with a man around

Phyllis Hurst. Laura Carter

nine-thirty that evening, and there and been sightings of various men in the area who became suspects, but were either eliminated or disappeared into the night and were never found.

The one recurrent image, and possibly a leading suspect, was that of a man seen in the area, and then spotted again twice in Halifax on the same evening; once a man fitting his description was seen on a bus passing Savile Park, and again he was seen near the junction of Skircoat and the Huddersfield road out of the town. He was never traced.

The description of this man was given as being aged twenty to twenty-five, short in height (around five feet five), clean shaven and with black hair combed straight back. He was wearing a fawn raincoat and brown shoes. Such a man was seen initially leaving a bus at Fairbank Road. In terms of the local geography, and of the man being seen again in Halifax later, this leads nowhere in particular. Two other men seen on the evening were, in fact, traced and interviewed, one even traced to Liverpool, but nothing came from these investigations either.

Phyllis had been savagely attacked, and in the language of the time, she was 'outraged' in this attack. The word implies some kind of sexual action but not necessarily rape. The word was used by the Chief Constable at the time, Thomas Rawson. All kinds of theories were put forward, and in the context of the burgeoning science of forensic psychology, the 'experts' consulted at the time had a field-day explaining the character

Officers during the investigation. Laura Carter

Mrs Mary O'Brien: she thought she had a suspect in mind. Laura Carter

of the killer being hunted. A 'consultant psychiatrist' suggested a profile: 'The mind of the offender in a case like this shows great disturbance. He is grossly immature, especially where sexual matters are concerned ... He turns to young children to gratify his needs ....' Such reporting and speculation led to what media analysts would call a 'moral panic' so that, for instance, one woman reported seeing 'a face at the window'. A crowd gathered in Portland Street, close to where the girl was found, because a woman passing by said that she saw a sheet of brown paper in an empty house, with a dull light behind it. This proved to be unsubstantiated.

The main lead was linked to sightings of a man with a bicycle; he was seen by several people at the time and a detailed description of the bike was given. The main suspicion fell on this because, as it was worded in the report, 'On the handlebars and frame was a bulky sack of irregular shape. The mouth of the sack was tied with white material.' The type of cycle was clearly defined: it was an old type,' with black frame and black mudguards, black rims and raised handlebars. The frame size was around twenty-two inches.'

We are left with a whole range of possibilities in the Hirst case. Three men were seen with a group of young girls in the two streets adjoining the lane where Phyllis was found; the cyclist was seen standing at the end of the lane, and then later, he was seen cycling towards the city centre. Finally, we have the mystery man who hopped on a bus and who appears to have made for Halifax with some alacrity. Inspector Gordon Wild, busy on the case most of the time, felt increasing frustration and confusion as time went on.

The facts are simple but lead to no known closure: a little girl went out to play and never came back home; she was attacked elsewhere and brought to the lane where she was found late on

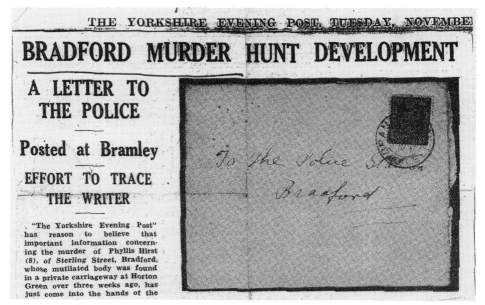

THE YORKSHIRE EVENING POST, TUESDAY, NOVEMBE[

BRADFORD MURDER HUNT DEVELOPMENT

A LETTER TO THE POLICE

Posted at Bramley

EFFORT TO TRACE THE WRITER

"The Yorkshire Evening Post" has reason to believe that important information concerning the murder of Phyllis Hirst (8), of Sterling Street, Bradford, whose mutilated body was found in a private carriageway at Horton Green over three weeks ago, has just come into the hands of the

The letter to the police. The Yorkshire Evening Post

the Friday night, 28 October 1938. The Halifax connection takes us to sightings of a man whose physical details are paradoxically accounted for: one witness noted his dark coat, and others his fawn raincoat. The only common factor is that the man was short and with black hair. That could be any one of a thousand men around the area.

Someone, most likely the man seen with Phyllis by Mrs Mary O'Brien that night, took advantage of the dark, the situation and the opportunity, and took the life of a young girl as she played in the street, just after leaving her friend Mary Baylis. The seduction was probably sweets or fun, or simply a touch of that Svengali-like approach often made by killers who do not wish to appear what they are, but quite the opposite. Sadly, this cold case is beginning to look like a frozen one: frozen in its time, now far beyond even reliable oral history, and the records are unlikely to be augmented by any new material.

CHAPTER 30

A Shooting in Dudley Hill 1945

The bullet had been fired from close range.

There have been thousands of crimes of passion throughout history, and many of the murders done with a motive of a need to possess the object of affection are done with an assured sense of rightness. But one of Bradford's most notorious killings in this category gives as a tale of a man who coolly shot his rival in a doorway with this exchange taking place:

Samuel Gray: *May I ask who the hell you are?*
William Batty: *I am nobody*

The shot was fired, and Gray, the soldier husband of Nellie, dropped dead in his own home. Batty, the man who pulled the trigger, had been calm and normal when playing dominoes with Albert Leeming in the *Cross Keys* on the evening before he left to kill his victim.

There had been a steady build-up to this bloody climax. Batty had been passing the time with Mrs Gray while her husband was fighting for his country in the Burma campaign. But the 'passing time' had really only been in Batty's mind. He had said a few words to her, and longed for her from a distance, creating a fantasy in his mind of having her to himself.

On 9 August, the soldier was about to be home on leave, and he wrote to Nellie to tell her the good news; somehow Batty learned of this, and the implication is that he conceived an extreme and desperate scheme to have her for himself and to remove the obstacle to his 'love'. He loitered around the house in Prince Street, Dudley Hill, and he had even boldly walked up

Samuel Gray, shot dead at his door. Laura Carter

to knock on the door on the night after Gray's arrival from the Far East. He had the door shut in his face by Nellie.

Batty's next move was to stare at the house from across the road, and then to ask a girl passing by, Alice Spilsbury, if she would knock on the Gray's door and tell the lady there that there was someone waiting to talk to her. There is no doubt that the lady inside knew who was out there. She was watching him with some trepidation, through her curtains, trying to pretend there was no problem. But there was a problem, and Alice sensed it, because she ran away when asked to knock at the door. This was four days before the killing, and what Batty was up to was messing around with his Luger pistol, something simmering inside him. Alice had heard him shoot the gun, and that was why she ran away.

The only option open to the man now that he had been rebuffed was to go straight to the house himself, and so he did. This time he was confronted by Gray, who asked to speak to the man's wife. His statement, 'I would like to talk to Nellie' led to the fatal exchange. Reckless is too restrained a word to use here: there were people who saw the shot fired. Mrs Ripley, next door, heard everything that happened and that was said. After the murder, as Batty panicked and ran, he was seen by James Sefton and his wife.

Samuel Gray was on the floor, his life ebbing away, and his neighbour ran in desperation to fetch help. It was a futile move. The bullet had been fired from close range. A photograph of the scene of crime shows the hapless Gray flat on his back, his broad, studded boots splayed wide, and the plain domestic scene of table and vase behind him. It is a recurring image of a domestic killing over the years. But in this case the 'crime of passion' was something spun from the fantasy of a loner, a man of only twenty-seven who played with guns just as foolishly as he played with his own fanciful imaginings. The killer could only think of one place to hide: his mother's house in Ireton Street. He arrived to find a welcome – but from the police, not his mother. His date with the hangman – 8 January 1946 – was already in motion.

It was a planned, determined killing and the execution of the killer would be as plain and quick as his own execution of Private Samuel Gray, who had left a war zone in which he had avoided death at the hands of the Japanese army, only to come home and die.

CHAPTER 31

A Lodging House Killing 1954

... a callous and nasty death.

Hangman Steve Wade had just learned his trade early in 1954, when he had attended to his first client at Armley Gaol: Albert Hall, who had killed little Mary Hackett in Halifax. He would only have to wait another five months for his second criminal, and this was Edward Reid, a Bradford character with a drink problem and a violent side. It is a teasing question to speculate how differently he would feel about his tasks: the child-killer and the drunkard who lost control and killed his room-mate. In theory, one might expect more sympathy for the man 'in his cups' who had a crazy moment and took a life, but at that time, the law was much more straightforward on capital punishment, and in Bradford it had been a callous and nasty death.

Reid shared a room with Arthur White in Mrs Fairweather's lodgings in Great Horton Road. It was a part of town where there were lodging houses; the number of labourers coming and going was always high and the demand for bed and board was strong. Men were thrown together, and if they didn't get on, it was hard luck. But there was a cause for tension between these two men. On 3 April, there was something more than ordinarily unpleasant brewing between them. As they ate their evening meal, the landlady said that there had been strong words at table. Whatever the cause of friction, going out to fill up with drink would not exactly help matters, and they both came home the worse for wear, White coming in very late, after Reid had arrived just after turning-out time.

When the body of White was found in the yard later, by another lodger, it looked as though it was a case of the drunk falling out of a third-floor window. But as the officer, Constable Priestly, went to look at White's room, he found a dishevelled and incoherent Reid there, and the man had blood on his face. In fact, the description of the scene is like a macabre version of the aftermath of two children playing with a sharp tool: blood smeared around and marks on the face: nothing very subtle when it comes to a criminal investigation. Everything pointed to a fight, and a very violent one too. The officer assumed that Reid had struck White and lost control, beating him to death, then throwing him outside to make it look like an accident.

Reid was going to find it hard to avoid this interpretation of events being accepted by detectives, despite his pathetic attempts, under interrogation, to claim that he had never set about his room-mate at all. After all, he had a swollen fist and said that he had injured his hand at work, labouring. When charged he said that he had 'Nowt to do with murder.' The blood on his arm and face had to come from somewhere and it matched White's. Added to that is the statement given by Mrs Fairweather that when Reid came home from the pub there had been no blood on him at all, certainly not on his face. It was not looking good for the man with the rash temper.

The only surprise is that it took the jury quite a while to decide: almost an hour. In September, Steve Wade and his assistant Harry Smith witnessed a rare sight: Edward Reid in a sober condition. Whether he was in a temper, there is no record to show.

CHAPTER 32

The 'Safe House' Murder 1954

... there had been a violent and bloody confrontation ...

Winston Shaw was a dangerous man. He liked to use his fists and to create fear. But he was one of those men who preferred to do these things to women, and one woman in particular felt his wrath: Jean Tate. First she had been his mistress and then his joint-partner when he lived with both her and his first wife; finally, she was his victim, when he took her life.

The *ménage a trois* had settled in Bradford and shared a flat, but it all became too much, and he left his two children with his wife, Florence, while he and Jean started afresh in Cunliffe Terrace, Manningham. It was a wild and volatile personality that Jean had to live with; he had no regular work and he had always had a nasty, aggressive side to him. He had promised to change, and she trusted him. The case became a template for so many sad relationships of this kind, because eventually, in desperation, Jean called for help. Shaw had started to treat her so despicably that he was shutting her in the flat when he left, and beating her up when he came home.

In November she brought in the police and even the NSPCC. The only sensible move was to find a safe house for her, and she was placed in Knareborough Hospital, in a flat meant for that purpose. But Shaw had all the time he needed to track her down, and he arrived at the flat to find that there were two officers present. From that point the story has a certain inevitable tragic fate attached to it. This is because there was no legal power with the officers giving them the scope for full protection of their charge. They could walk him out of the place and tell

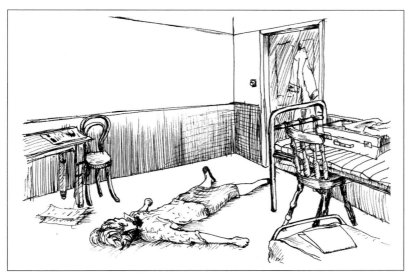

Jean Tate's body in her 'safe' flat. Laura Carter

him not to go back, but that was the end of it. He then loitered around, waiting for his chance.

Only a matter of a few hours after he was escorted out, neighbours heard screams from Jean. One woman who lived close and who knew Jean's precarious situation was the person who found her body. Jean was lying on the floor, on her back, with severe injuries to her head and chest. The scene of crime pictures show that there had been a violent and bloody confrontation, and that the victim had been dragged inside the room.

Shaw was staying nearby and was visited by police later that night. From then on, clues were soon found. Shaw actually had a bloody axe-head in the room, and a knife. When he learned that she was dead he simply said, 'She has ruined me and now she has brought me to this.' Further investigation revealed that he had hidden the knife the police were looking for, behind some skirting boards. The widow in the next flat gave a graphic account of the results of Shaw's fury. She said that she heard Jean's voice shout, 'God, help! He's got me!' Then she said, 'I heard a thud, and I heard some quick footsteps going downstairs. I went out on the landing and saw a pool of blood on the floor. This was running out of Jean's flat ....'

These stairs were stained with Tate's blood.
Laura Carter

A nurse passed shortly after this, and the woman shouted to her that Jean had been murdered. The nurse also went in and saw the body, felt sure that Jean was dead, and then rang the police.

In court, forensic reports tied the two weapons clearly to the inflicted wounds. The victim had been stabbed twenty times in the neck. The axe had been hacked into her head five times. The pathologist confirmed what the photographs show: Jean had been attacked on the landing and dragged inside. Shaw's weak attempts to explain possession of the weapons were so laughably ineffectual that he clearly knew he had no chance of surviving this trial. Knaresborough retailers had confirmed that Shaw had bought the weapons in the town. The killer's story that he bought the knife from a boy scout was something from a child's comic, as it was so threadbare and obviously

The bathroom in the flat. The killer was heard using 'a lot of water' here. Laura Carter

untrue. It was a cock-and-bull story about his remorse, even to the point of seeing what he had done and kissing her on the forehead. The more Shaw said, the more he was digging a pit for himself. He had patently invented another man and put him in the murder scene, suggesting that Jean had some other passionate entanglement leading to violence by another, nameless man.

He even tried to say that another man was in the room, attacking Jean, and that Jean had pushed herself between the two men. As the judge said in his summing-up, why would a man who had shoved Shaw to the ground then pick up a knife and stab the victim twenty times with it? There is a crazy and dark comic irony in Shaw's statement, 'If that is the jury's verdict, then I accept it.' This was said as if he had any choice in the matter.

It took the jury just forty-five minutes to decide on a guilty verdict. The trial had lasted three days, largely because of the ridiculous narrative concocted as one of the weakest defences ever recorded in a murder case. Shaw was hanged on 4 May 1955.

CHAPTER 33

The Gas Meter Case
1957

... a rash and desperate act by a man who was hard up.

In May 1957, the Appeal Court had to decide on a particularly tricky legal situation. As so often happens, the business all hinged on whether a man had intended to cause harm, with a wicked design. The discussion took some considerable time, and it all started with the theft of cash from a gas meter.

Roy Cunningham was strapped for cash in January 1957. The best idea he could conceive to gather some money was to go to 7A Bakes Street in Bradford, a house that was being rented for him by his future mother-in-law. Cunningham smashed the meter, wrenched it from the wall and took it away. He took it to where he could access the contents and make as much noise as he had to. That was a crime of larceny. But the problem was that, as he ripped the machine out, he fractured a gas main.

This fracture led to gas escaping through a cellar wall and into the next-door property. Sarah Wade was lying asleep at that time and, of course, she breathed in quite a large quantity of gas. Sarah was very seriously ill and was lucky to survive. The point about Cunningham's actions was that he might have been expected to be aware of what had happened, and in fact there was a stop-tap only a few feet away from the meter. He did not turn this off.

In court, Cunningham pleaded guilty to larceny and was given a custodial sentence of six months. The sentence took into account the fact that what he had done caused a real danger to life. The point at issue at the appeal hearing was then whether or not there was anything malicious in the action that led to, what the judge called, 'a frightful cloud of coal gas' being inhaled by the luckless Mrs Wade.

As it was certain Cunningham did not know he had fractured the gas main, it should not have been too difficult to sort things out. But Cunningham's lawyer had to go a long way back in legal history to find a precedent that would serve him well. This was a case in 1874 in which a man had thrown a brick into a crowd of people, intending to hit a person with the brick, but had unintentionally broken a glass window. The point of law was all about the kind of intended harm in each case.

The important information now ascertained was about the actual nature of the houses in question. The two houses concerned had, at one time, been only one property. When the place was converted into semi-detached dwellings, a wall had been constructed between the cellars, but this was a very rough piece of work, simply being rubble only loosely cemented together. In terms of the criminal law, everything came down to whether there was a felony involving an intention to harm another person. The stop-tap was not turned off because Cunningham had no idea of what he had actually done on breaking the machine. Therefore he had no intention to do harm, and also had not done anything with a reckless awareness of possible risk to another.

Cunningham explained what he had done in a very forthright way: 'All right, I will tell you ... I was short of money. I had been off work for three days. I got eight shillings from the gas meter. I tore it off the wall and threw it away.' This does have some recklessness if he was aware of the elderly neighbours, and of the likely consequences of what he had done.

The prosecution interpreted the larceny in that way, suggesting that Cunningham must have known the likely consequences. It was said that 'he must have known perfectly well that gas would percolate all over the house ....' Things might have deteriorated for the man responsible for all this mayhem, but he was redeemed by a point of law – that the judge at the initial trial directed the jury, using the word 'malicious'. Naturally, he should not have done that, as there had been no description of what he had done that made the theft malicious in any way. It was simply a rash and desperate act by a man who was hard up.

The conviction was quashed. We have to wonder, though, what kind of man his mother-in-law was allowing into her family. Cunningham's future wife was remarkably silent through all this.

CHAPTER 34

The Deadly Syringe 1957

... the forensic team still had some thinking to do ...

In 1984, on being released from prison, nurse Kenneth Barlow still insisted that he had not killed his wife, back in 1957. He had served a life sentence, if not to the letter then according to the current sentencing procedure. Barlow had set the forensic experts a real conundrum almost thirty years before, and though it is virtually certain that he poisoned his wife with an insulin overdose, the discussion goes on.

In conversation with a colleague during his medical career, Barlow had said, 'Anyone gets a load of this, and it's the quickest way out.' He was talking about insulin, and one of his regular tasks was to administer such substances. It was no surprise to the police, then, in 1957, to find two hypodermic syringes in his home when they were called out to investigate the death of his wife, on 3 May.

This was a suspicious death that began as a plain tale of possible death due to illness – hypoglycemia – but there were factors in Barlow's account of the circumstances of the death which raised questions. The doctor who was called, and later the police who listened to Barlow's account, heard a story that began with Mrs Barlow being ill and going to have a bath. She died in that bath, and her husband claimed that he had frantically tried to revive her. He said she had been ill for hours, being sick and suffering a high temperature. He had slept as she bathed and found her under water when he woke up. But the doctor noted that Elizabeth's pupils were dilated and this was odd, so he brought the police in.

From that point, there were other oddities. The doctor had seen that water was in the elbow-cups of her body; this was strange if there had been a struggle; more obviously, why were Barlow's pyjamas perfectly dry? He said that he had tried desperately to revive her, so he would have been very wet. When asked why he had the syringes, Barlow explained that he had been suffering from a carbuncle and had been using the needles to treat himself.

Medical examination initially could find no apparent reason, despite her being two month's pregnant, why Mrs Barlow should have fainted. But Dr Price began a long and exhaustive inspection of the corpse to find any punctures caused by syringes. Finally, he did find them: two tiny marks on each buttock. The red marks around them indicated that they had been recently done. The only problem now was to discover what had been in the syringe.

Enter more experts from the Home Office Forensic Service. The basis of the supposed illness and cause of death could have been hypoglycaemia, so if she had been given a massive insulin dose, everything would be satisfactorily explained. But that would mean a very low blood sugar level, and tests showed that her levels were very high. Insulin had never been used as a murder method, so new ground was being trodden here, and things escalated when police learned that he had talked about insulin being used to commit the 'perfect murder.'

But the forensic team still had some thinking to do, and it was realised that, as there was no standard test for establishing insulin in the body, it was recalled that the liver will tend to flood the body with sugar before death. This could have happened, so how to establish this was the next question. Tests were done on mice, giving them massive doses, and then extracts from the tissue of Mrs Barlow's body were given to other mice: both groups behaved in the same way: the creatures were intensely hot and nervous, went into a coma and eventually died. This was a process that mirrored Mrs Barlow's death very closely. They were almost there, but there was still one obstacle in their way if they were to show what the suspect had done.

This was the well-known fact that insulin went from the body very quickly. But luck was on the side of the scientists, as lactic acid, produced in the muscle, remained static after death and acted to preserve the insulin. This was the last piece in the jigsaw. Barlow was questioned more actively and began admitting various treatments he had administered to his wife. There was a case to answer, and now the business could go to court.

There was a strong enough case to show wilful murder, and so a life sentence was imposed. When Kenneth Barlow walked out a free man, twenty-one years ago as I write, he must have rued saying those rash words to his workmate. After all, a suspect with medical knowledge is always going to be scrutinised more carefully than the layperson in any murder investigation. Forensic science cornered this killer, although good detective work helped to raise the important questions at an early stage in the investigation.

CHAPTER 35

A Murder and a Tape-Recording 1965

They had shown no mercy ...

In 1964, Maqsud Ali and Ashiq Hussain were convicted of murder at Leeds Assizes. Melford Stevenson had sentenced them to life imprisonment and deportation for killing Nasim Akhtar in April that year. The story of that killing is straightforward enough. But it is what happened at the appeal hearing that is of real interest, and those events take over the narrative interest at the heart of the case.

The murder itself is in that sadly familiar category of the honour killing, featured so prominently recently in cases such as Tasleem Begum and Heshu Jones. These are, as one reporter has said, 'affairs of the heart that end in tragedy.' On 7 December 2004, the *Daily Telegraph* reported that 122 cases such as these are to be reviewed. Police and the Crown Prosecution Service were to ask coroners for suspected cases that might be in this category.

Nasim Akhtar must be one of the earliest victims. It was a savage murder. The two had been merciless to their victim, and it had been one more depressingly familiar attack on a defenceless woman. They had shown no mercy and in their minds they had justified the killing in such a way that it related to the morality of a culture very different from that of their adopted country. Nasim had no chance of escape.

But it was at the appeal that the story became particularly intriguing, as it was all about admissible evidence, and the story is that, when both men were brought to a room in Bradford Town Hall, with a police officer and a Pakistani liaison officer,

Bradford Town Hall where the tape-recording took place. The author

they were left to talk alone in a room that had been bugged. A tape recorder was set up, with only the police having knowledge of this. For just over an hour the men spoke, but they spoke in a specific Punjabi dialect.

Although the jury at the appeal hearing had a transcript of the conversation, there were several questionable elements here. First, was it an action on the part of the law that could be condoned and allowed to be used as evidence? Second, all through the talk there had been intermittent noise from traffic, and there was an open window in the room; there was a bus-stop down below, under that window. This had been used as part of the process of information-gathering to convict the men.

As if this were not enough to complicate affairs, the point arose in court that there were significant problems with translation issues. The defence lawyers argued that the whole business was a travesty of justice: it was a bad recording; several people had been involved in the translation, and they tried to dismiss the legality of the act.

But it had been done before. As one report commented: 'The method of the informer and of the eavesdropper had been used before in the detection of crime.' When the two men had gone to the Town Hall they had not been coerced, and indeed they were not in custody. The judge saw no difference between a photograph and a tape, and talked about a case earlier that year in which a tape had been allowed in court (in Nottingham).

In this case, then, we have not only a murder that is sickeningly familiar in the culture of certain ethnic groups, but also a remarkable instance of extreme methods being used to trap perpetrators of extreme, nasty and violent crimes.

CHAPTER 36

Vicious Attack in the *Barracks Tavern* 1965

It all spun out of control ...

Mohammed Akbar would come to rue the day he walked into the *Barracks Tavern* in Bradford, in May 1965. The pub, on Killinghall Road, was close to the location of the city barracks and had been rebuilt in the late 1920s in a mock-Tudor style. It is no longer standing, but when Akbar walked in for a drink, he was going into what seemed outwardly like a typical corner-pub in city suburbs.

In truth, that is exactly what it was, but there were two sisters drinking in there on that night, and one of them had a grudge against Mr Akbar. At first it was a case of an insult passed and some scowling, but it soon escalated. Elizabeth and Kathleen Duffy were in a mood for a fight, and the unfortunate publican was to see a most unseemly brawl break out in his lounge bar. The confrontation happened very quickly, as the landlord stated in court that he never saw Kathleen Duffy break a glass, but she did so, and within seconds, when he glanced at the man involved, there was blood all over his face and chest. Kathleen had cut him, and with a malicious intent.

Soon the two of them were on the floor, struggling, and Elizabeth, who had been in the toilet, came out to join in. She grabbed a bottle and hit Akbar on the head with it, and with considerable force. A witness, Mr Hant, said that he saw Akbar 'holding on to Kathleen Duffy' and that she repeatedly slashed him with a glass.

Two constables were soon on the scene and Elizabeth must have been very determined to do some harm, as she fought on,

The Barracks Tavern. Laura Carter

even with the police now present. It all spun out of control, and it never became entirely clear what the 'grudge' was.

In court, Kathleen said that she had struck Akbar, but then that he had aimed a glass at her, cutting her hand. This drove her into a fury. Her main defence was that she was very drunk on that occasion and had no real awareness of how furiously she had attacked the man. Elizabeth's testimony was different from the landlord's. In her version, she had come from the toilet and seen Akbar tugging at her sister's hair, as Kathleen was crouching on her knees. She also claimed that he had kicked her hard on the leg as she struggled to pull him away from her sister.

There is no doubt that Akbar came off the worst: he had severe facial lacerations. He had been, as it is usually expressed in the context of a drunken fight, 'glassed.' Everything seemed clear, however, to the judge at the first hearing. He saw no case for self-defence in mitigation of Elizabeth Duffy's actions with the bottle. The judge's argument for this decision was that there was no precedent example of a sister using force to defend her sister in such circumstances. Through modern eyes, this seems a very strange and irrational point, and the judge appears to have made up his mind about the truth of the events at the Barrack that night.

At the initial trial, the judge had said, 'There is no suggestion whatever that she personally was attacked and it is my direction to you to approach this case on the footing that it is no defence for Lilian (Elizabeth) Duffy to say she was going to the assistance of her sister.'

Of course, even with the judge keeping out of the decision-making process, the jury may have decided that the evidence pointed to a malicious and unprovoked attack on Akbar, but that counted for nothing at the appeal hearing. Elizabeth Duffy was discharged and the sentence quashed. In effect, the fight in the *Barracks Tavern* was like every other brawl on record: two people very much drunk and disorderly, and then being incited to violence by some normally small insult or perceived antagonism. It was only because the judge did not allow the course of events to flow as they would when perceptions were blurred that an appeal followed.

CHAPTER 37

Another Brave Officer
1970

This was a ruthless man they were now looking for.

The police force Roll of Honour is a text perhaps not so well-known to the general public. Police officers risk their lives every day for their communities. Most regions of Britain have their local instances of this, and when we read the story of how Inspector Barry Taylor died in 1970 it brings home the vulnerability of officers, when when they are not working alone. He was a married man with two children, and he had been in the police force for almost ten years when he came across a hardened killer.

The incident happened at Sunny Bank Mills, in the Pudsey district, and not long after midnight officers at Pudsey responded to the building alarm buzzer from the textile mill. There were factors known to them that would have helped them to act in the right way, such as the knowledge that there would be two men on the premises: a watchman near the main gate and an engineer who lived towards the back of the site.

The keys, a crucial element in acting to investigate, were in the possession of this engineer.

Thirty-year-old Inspector Taylor was on patrol and his radio picked up the alarm, so he went straight to the mills, collecting another officer on his way. Another car had arrived just before him, so there were several constables there, and Taylor took charge, going inside on his own, and leaving the others to observe. The main expectation would be for anyone in there who should not be there to exit smartly. He did the obvious thing: walked to talk to the engineer and get the keys, then they both walked into the mill yard. But they disturbed Neil

Adamson, a violent man who was there, and he was armed. He wasted no time in firing at the inspector, and Taylor, now at the front gates, was shot dead. Adamson ran away in haste; the officers did not see or go in pursuit.

Adamson had already killed: he had shot the watchman, whose body was found in his office; so he had nothing to lose in shooting again, and asking questions later. This was a ruthless man they were now looking for. He had shot the watchman at close range, twice in the head. It only took two days to trace the killer, though. He was traced to Colne and arrested there.

Neil Adamson was a very dangerous man, and had been a dangerous youth as well; he had been in and out of prison for crimes against the person, including grievous bodily harm and wounding. Now he had graduated to the status of murderer. There was some deep malaise in the man, and he had been to seek help from doctors, but nothing really significant had been done to treat him. He was a 'walking time bomb' and Inspector Taylor happened to be there when he exploded.

The killer pleaded guilty and was given a life sentence of thirty years, as there had been guilt on two counts of murder.

CHAPTER 38

Threats and Rabid Murder 1975

... he wanted to 'beat Neilson'.

The Home Office Criminal Statistics for the decade up to 1980 show that there were thirty-four killings by mentally disturbed people in 1970, and thirty-nine in 1980. Mark Rowntree, from Guiseley, contributed significantly to those statistics. But no-one connected with the unlucky victims of his rage would want to hear the word 'statistics' in that context.

Rowntree is now held now in St Luke's Hospital in Middlesborough. His bloody history began when he was just nineteen and about to go to university. He was walking in Bingley and as he passed a house in Old Main Street, he noticed the outline of a person through a window; this was eighty-five-year-old widow, Grace Adamson. She had been a dance teacher and photographs of her show that she was still fit and athletic at this stage in her life. Neighbours talked about her as 'a sweet old soul'. But there was nothing sweet about her death. Rowntree simply knocked on her door and as she opened the door to face him he set about her with a knife. This was on New Year's Eve.

Mark Rowntree.
Laura Carter

But the killing spree was on Rowntree and he did not stop there. He had been reading about the Bradford killer Donald Neilson, the so-called Black Panther, who had killed three sub-postmasters between 1971 and 1975. Rowntree was merely selecting his victims at random. He

Stephen Wilson. Laura Carter

later explained his actions by saying that he wanted to 'beat Neilson.'

He arrived in Keighley just three days later, and found himself in Eastburn, where sixteen-year-old Stephen Wilson was waiting for a bus. Stephen was from a large family, and was a hard-working young man who was aiming to go into nursing. Rowntree again selected him just on a whim when the 'right moment' came, and stabbed him to death. Wilson did manage to survive for a short while, even struggling to go to a house close by and try to find help. He managed to give information to police before he died.

Rowntree was living on the edge of society; he wandered and liked to be anonymous in these periods of homicidal power, emerging to kill unexpectedly, in a frenzy. According to the *Yorkshire Post* he had sometimes paid for sex, and one person who had experienced him as a client was to pay the ultimate price as his murder ride drove on. This time it was in Burley, and he arrived at the home of Barbara Booth to kill her and her young son, Alan. The toddler was stabbed fifteen times.

Barbara Booth. Laura Carter

How can we even begin to explain such a mental illness and its terrifying expression? Rowntree had wealthy parents (who had adopted him when he was a baby) and went to very good schools. He did manage to follow the route through schools, eventually to Rishworth School, near Halifax. But he always had violent tendencies. One of the most useful statements about how such destructive urges come to exist has been put by Peter Shaffer, in his play, *Equus*: 'A child is born into a world of phenomena, all equal in their

Grace Anderson. Laura Carter

power to enslave. ... Suddenly one strikes. Why? Moments snap together like magnets, forging a chain of shackles.' One of these moments 'struck' Mark Rowntree and it was in his dark interior life.

That unknown factor that creates what the media call 'a homicidal maniac' is beyond definition. He was officially classified as a paranoid schizophrenic according to the *Yorkshire Post*, his life after the crimes being a round of periods spent in hospitals such as Broadmoor and Rampton. But sensation and shock have dogged everything about this man. In 1994 he was allowed to participate in and adventure holiday in Keilder Forest, Northumberland. That was something for which the Home Secretary at the time had to apologise.

In the end, attempts to explain this version of murder, which causes killers to be detained indefinitely, always meet the paradox that the killers can often stand back and explain the acts they do. Rowntree is no exception. He has explained his murders with these words: 'I am able to transcend any moral feelings of responsibility or obligations.' More significantly, he has also said, 'I am not at all angry, nor am I disturbed or mad; I feel quite rational, calm and balanced in mind.'

In the annals of the history of murder in our society, such puzzles keep on coming up to challenge and confuse the everyday workings of police investigation. As far as the relatives of victims are concerned, though, all the theory in the world cannot bring back a loved one who just happened to be in the wrong place at the wrong time.

CHAPTER 39

The Body in the River 1977

The search began and it was not pleasant.

The newspapers keep telling us how DNA advances have revolutionised forensic science, and how new, refined techniques are making it easier to track down killers. Few people would be as certain of this as Ian Lowther, who opened his door in April 2000, to be arrested for a murder he committed twenty-three years earlier. Detectives stood at the door of his home in Baildon, confident that they had got their man.

Lowther had been working on a Laing building site, playing his part in the construction of the huge Inland Revenue centre at Shipley. His victim was Mrs Mary Gregson, who working at Salt's Mill, Saltaire, at the time. Mary was happily married, with a young son; she lived very close to Salt's Mill, and her husband, Bill, worked in Bingley. On a summer's day in August 1977 Mary Parker was walking along the Leeds-Liverpool Canal towpath on her way to work, where she was to cover for a friend who was ill. That night, as she had never met a friend at a given time, nor arrived at work, the family and friends were understandably worried. The search began and it was not pleasant.

The water of the River Aire where she was found (the canal and river run close together) is not exactly clean and pure. As police searched the area, one constable had the bad luck to find a handbag, and then to see a hand sticking up from the muddy water. Mary Gregson had been found. The horrible facts of the manner of her death emerged after a difficult medical examination. She had been brutally attacked and sexually assaulted. It was thought that her severe injuries were the result of being cracked against the ground repeatedly, and she had been punched. Before being thrown into the water, she had been strangled. After initial questioning around the place, the only profile of the killer was that he was likely to be white and between sixteen and forty.

One interesting lead came when an Italian woman arrived, with a priest as translator, to say that she had seen a man standing over the body. She gave his name as Jan; he had spoken to her quite freely and given his name. This surely made him an unlikely suspect. But the obvious first move was to interview the thousands of workers close by – both at Salt's Mill and on the construction site.

This was the beginning of a police investigation that must go down on record as one of the most painstaking, patient and dedicated ever undertaken in Britain. The interviews took a very long time. Other contemporary factors clouded the issue – mainly the minor detail that it all happened in what we now call 'The Yorkshire Ripper Years' when people in West Yorkshire were constantly talking about such a major moral panic that any other murder would either be thought of as another Ripper killing or as something less important.

Forensics had semen to work with. Much other material had been polluted in the acrid waters. January 1978 brought everything to a halt. It was a cul-de-sac and the hard work stopped – but only for the time being.

This takes the story to a number of years in which, while the hunt for the killer was not out of the police officers' thoughts, DNA research was going ahead steadily. The advance of Low Copy Number technique was emerging, and this meant that work could be done on tiny quantities of substances which might previously have been discounted from forensic work. Definitive murderer profiles were now possible, with an amazing one in a billion chance of two people sharing the same DNA characteristics. The officer in charge, DCS Taylor, has explained to crime writer Andy Owens how the work ahead, using the new material, was made easier by narrowing down the revisiting of files about interviews taken from construction workers all those years ago. He explained that of the eight hundred workers on the Inland Revenue site at the time, a figure of a first thousand was gathered from men who matched the theoretical type and offender profiling features. These were then given a buccal swab (saliva taken from inside the mouth, on the cheek).

In the first 1,000 swabs, they found a match. The next step was the drive to Baildon to arrest the man. He was still there, a man who had been happily married but had now set up in a new address and was living a quiet life, walking and working out at the gym. Neighbours said what a good man he was, a man who could be trusted to babysit. He had stayed in the area, kept up with developments on the case, and had even watched the BBC *Crimewatch* programme about the murder.

It seems that he was expecting the detectives; he had had a visit not long before when the routine recaps on previous interviews were going ahead. The judge in court must have secretly enjoyed saying these final words before Lowther was sentenced: 'Twenty-three years ago you robbed an innocent woman of her life. You robbed parents of a child, a husband of a wife, and a son of his mother ... all this loss and tragedy to satisfy a few minutes lust.'

Lust it had been: Lowther had, unusually for him, taken the day off work, drunk seven pints of beer, and taken a walk on the towpath. Twenty-three years later, he faced life imprisonment for what he did that day to a good woman walking to work.

CHAPTER 40

'Twenty-Four Years to Clear my Name' 1977

... a chapter of errors and confusion ...

We know a great deal about the last walk of Carole Wilkinson in October 1977, from leaving home in Ranelagh Avenue to the bakery in Gain Lane, Thornbury, where she worked. When she reached Woodhall Road, she was viciously attacked from behind and struck by a fifty-pound coping stone. This was nine o'clock in the morning; two days later, when classified as clinically dead, her parents had the awful task of allowing her life-support machine to be turned off. When found, she had been stripped and assaulted. Superficially, this could have looked like yet another Ripper killing.

It would prove to be a distraction from the hunt for the Ripper for Dennis Hoban of the CID, and most irritatingly for a hoax, as local children had said that a man with a blue anorak had done the attack. 'The man with the Blue Anorak' turned out to be such a hoax that it almost became something believed locally and entered into local urban mythology.

Carole Wilkinson. Laura Carter

That was one disastrous result of this crime. Another was far more serious, as it resulted in the wrongful conviction of a man who was finally released from gaol in March 2003 when his murder conviction was quashed. The man was Anthony Steel. On release, he told the press, referring to the real killer, 'I know this

The murder scene. Laura Carter

man. I saw him almost every day I was in Wakefield Prison. Long before I knew about any evidence that might link him to the crime I knew that he avoided me . . . .' What had happened for such a terrible ordeal to happen to an innocent man? At the time of the killing, there were no real suspects. But more than a year after, when there was no progress and the hoax had wasted police time, a phone call was received, and it named Steel as the owner of a fish-shaped key ring which was claimed to belong to the dead girl, and which had been seen in Steel's possession.

This seems like slender and questionable material with which to forge a link. But Steel was questioned, and for a period of several days, on and off, despite the fact that he had an alibi. The police, it is claimed, put together the narrative of the murder, and imposed it on the case: he had stalked the girl, and then pounced.

But however it came about, the nervous and vulnerable young gardener somehow made a confession, despite phone calls and letters from a woman who said her son had done the murder. The next stop was, inevitably, Leeds Crown Court, in December 1979. He was sentenced to life in prison. But, as with the more famous cases of Dennis Stafford and of The Torso in the Tank case, a BBC *Rough Justice* programme achieved what should have been done long before: searched out the truth as far as it was understood. This was in 1995, and the programme

Anthony Steel on his release. Laura Carter

examined the key ring 'evidence' and also the questionable interrogation.

This is where a major factor in the case becomes apparent, and it is beyond belief that this happened: Steel was suffering from a mental handicap at the time of his arrest. He had clearly not been able to cope and was not in possession of his faculties during those three long interviews. Steel actually stated that he was told that he could not have legal representation unless he signed a form placed in front of him: a confession. The central fact is that the 1979 jury had no information about this mental condition.

It has to be said, however, that top police detective Jim Hobson, was aware of a problem regarding the police handling of the case back at the time of the arrest. When he heard that Steel had signed a confession, he came to Pudsey police station to check that all was in order with this charge. The men conducting the case, while Hobson was working on the Ripper enquiry, insisted that they had enough on Steel for a murder charge. But Hobson had only limited information, despite his examination of Steel to check on special knowledge. Steel actually got some facts and details wrong, so there were slight doubts in Hobson's mind. The focus of this 'special knowledge' about Carol and the attack was her handbag. It was actually blue denim, but her brother and other people had said it was brown; Steel said it was brown. What was going on?

Perhaps the detectives hearing the statements had not checked the accounts written at the time, eighteen months before? These would have confirmed that the handbag was blue denim. Yet there was another fine detail. This concerned the girl's knickers and tights being pulled down. She was having a period and there was a bloodstained tampax by her body. Steel had no knowledge nor memory of any of this.

At the first appeal hearing in 1981, the statement of confession was discussed again, and Lord Justice Lane said, 'the statement had ... ample evidence for the jury to come to the conclusion that they did.' The police procedure, the muddle and mayhem of the Ripper Inquiry, and the mystery of the missing facts about Steel's mental condition, all add a very questionable dimension to this case. But now it is all history, unable to be changed. Bradford chronicles of crime will have to put the Steel case down to a terrible confusion, or more likely, a chapter of errors and circumstances, with a young man at the centre of it all who had his freedom taken away. In an account of the case written by Louise Pearce for *True Crime* magazine, Anthony Steel is shown in photographs with his sister and a friend. He is smiling, smartly dressed and relaxed. This is a powerful image of a man who claims he was forced to confess. We will never know the absolute truth, but one detail is arguably very significant: the man he saw in prison was convicted of rape, robbery and assault, to a total of twenty-eight charges, and he had been arrested on the footpath by Woodhall Road where Carole Wilkinson was attacked.

CHAPTER 41

Ripper Murders
1977–79

The file ... will inevitably go on.

On the chronicles of murder in the Bradford area, it surprises no-one to learn that the crimes committed by Peter Sutcliffe, the Yorkshire Ripper, tend to dominate the reference books, media coverage and web sites. In the poignant listings of his victims are three definite murders around Bradford: those of Tina Atkinson (1977), Yvonne Pearson (1978) and Barbara Leach (1979). But there are other attacks recorded, and other cases of probable connection to Sutcliffe, but not definitely recorded as such.

The career of the Yorkshire Ripper has the trajectory so often linked to that version of psychopath who has to begin with tentative approaches to possible victims, and gradually raise the risks and the excitement levels to the point at which a killing has to take place, and it has to be done in a certain way. In this case, one of the earliest attacks fortunately did not end in a death. This was in Keighley, early on the Saturday morning,

A scene during the Barbara Leach investigation. Laura Carter

5 July 1975, when Anna Rogulskyj was viciously attacked from behind. She had been cracked with a hammer three times and was amazingly still alive – but only just – and she was rushed to hospital. It was then found that she had also been cut across the stomach. It took a twelve-hour operation to save her life.

In 1974, it seems highly likely that there was a Ripper attack in Bradford, this one on Gloria Wood, and she also survived. Gloria was a student at the time and on 11 November, as she was walking across a school field, she met a man who seemed kind, as she was laden down with heavy bags and he said he would help. But she says that he began to strike her with a claw-hammer. She only survived because there were people nearby who disturbed the ritual that the Ripper needed. Gloria's description of the assailant was that he was medium height, with a short curly beard and dark hair, wearing a dark suit. Her skull was fractured, and she was clearly very close to being on the list of murder victims.

There are other possible victims beginning to be recorded and discussed, mainly due to a television programme, broadcast in 1996, *Silent Victims: The Untold Story of the Yorkshire Ripper*. The documentary dealt with six attacks and most of these seem highly likely to be put down as Sutcliffe cases. Gloria Wood's attack was perhaps the most obvious one to link to him, but there are other brief accounts, maybe all part of the sequence in that early phase, when he was gaining a twisted kind of confidence in his sick and brutal regime.

In August 1976, for instance, a housewife in Lister Hills was attacked in the early hours of the morning: she was stabbed in the stomach. Earlier, in 1972, according to Keith Hellawell in his book of memoirs, an Irish student was attacked in Bradford, as reported at the time. Yet the documentary attaches the crime to Leeds. The tendency is for crime historians to want to link any brutal murder committed around the Leeds–Bradford conurbation in these years to the Ripper. Even some murders which have no features of a Ripper attack have been suggested, such as the unsolved murder of Mary Judge near Leeds Parish Church in 1968, which is clearly not the work of Sutcliffe.

But in the facts around the murder of Tina Atkinson on 23 April 1977 there is no doubt about the identity of the killer.

Moving closer: the yard near where Leach was found. Laura Carter

She was a divorced mother who worked as a prostitute, based in a flat, and she returned home one day to find the Ripper there, making all circumstances easy for him to strike. Tina had had a great deal to drink, and had enjoyed a pub crawl looking for business. When she left the Carlisle pub just after ten on a warm Saturday evening she was noticed. She carried on working for a while, then went to her flat.

The next day, early evening, one of her close friends went to check on her and to have a chat; he was to find her mutilated body on the bed. The pathologist on the scene, Dr Gee, was the first medical man to have to write up a report of what was to become a sickeningly familiar tale across Yorkshire: a chisel had been used, and she had been stabbed in the body and neck. She had not been raped. It is staggering to note just how much alcohol was in her body – twenty spirit measures – and we have to wonder how much she knew about anything that went on that night, particularly as she was struck as soon as she entered the room.

In January 1978, Yvonne Pearson's body was found under a dumped sofa in a waste site. This was perhaps the most disgustingly brutal attack, as she had been struck so violently and relentlessly on her skull, and that had fragmented into twenty-one pieces. To do this nasty work of destruction, a heavy ball-hammer had been used. As a final humiliation, some old stuffing

The old sofa where Yvonne Pearson's body was found. Laura Carter

material from the sofa had been rammed into her gullet. This time, there was nothing to denote the usual stabbing, but the hammer and the sexual elements to the killing pointed to the Ripper. Ironically, Yvonne had been heard to say on one occasion, 'It would be just my luck to meet the Ripper.'

At this stage, the operation to catch the killer was being increased and more men deployed. In April 1979, the event happened that was to divert the investigations and arguably made the last killings more manageable for the Ripper: this was the arrival of the Wearside Jack tapes, sent to George Oldfield who led the investigation. Valuable time was spent in gathering experts and scholars to study the tape and to trace the location of the speaker, as he had a distinct Wearside accent. The focus shifted from West Yorkshire to Castletown near Sunderland. Though the general paranoia about the identity of the Ripper went on, there was less intense concentration on the Bradford conurbation.

During this period the eleventh victim was found: student Barbara Leach had enjoyed a night out at the *Manville Arms* in Bradford. After this she decided to walk home alone: just the thing that the police had been advising women not to do. She only managed to walk around twenty yards before he struck. Student flatmates assumed she was sleeping somewhere else, but they were worried the next day. Her body was found under an old carpet, in an alley. Bricks had been piled on this. The scene provided the usual degrading and seedy atmosphere, as he chose to haunt the back alleys and yards of the northern towns.

Barbara had even asked a flatmate to wait up for her. She had said that she just wanted a walk, after stepping out of the pub into Great Horton Road. It was a quarter to one. The search for her took a few days, and there was still a faint hope that she might turn up for an appointment that had been made for 12.30 on the next Monday. She never arrived and not long after, a constable found the body. It was a shocking experience for PC Simon Greaves.

It is instructive to look back at those years with the knowledge of hindsight, and to be aware of David Canter's concept of mapping in profile work. It all looks so simple now: thirteen murders and at least eleven attacks, all within a twenty mile radius of Bradford's centre (with the exception of the Manchester killing). It all points to a person living close to Bradford, taking the excursions to places he could reach within a set period of time, and from where he could return to his lair smoothly and quickly.

The file on other potential victims of the Sutcliffe campaign will inevitably go on. The documents linked to the Byford Report on the way the police dealt with the case had some spin-offs in this ongoing investigation, and the author of *Wicked Beyond Belief*, a full story of the Yorkshire Ripper by Michael Bilton, makes use of these documents. This suggests that anything else likely to emerge now that might be related to these murders will be marginal and perhaps difficult to substantiate.

CHAPTER 42

Salts of Lemon: A Sad Story 1914

... he had no intention of killing himself ...

As with every other place on earth, among rich or poor, Bradford has had its share of suicide, and it is a melancholy fact that until 1961, suicide and attempted suicide were criminal offences. The more common way to leave this life at one's own hands is illustrated in the tragic but brief account of the death of Louis Beecher in 1850. Here, a young man had been in Beecher's house and found him apparently quite well, but the clerk working for Messrs Swabe and Co, then put two pistols to his head and ended it all. All we know from the bare report of this is that 'He was a native of Saxony, and about thirty-two years of age'.

This is all very complete and typical, but what can we say about a man who tried to kill himself using salts of lemon? John William Mann had suffered two stretches in prison for attempted suicide when he was arrested on a tramcar in a poor condition, not only drunk but, according to medical statements, showing the effects of taking salts of lemon. Mann vehemently claimed that he had no intention of killing himself, and that may be so, as there would have been several reasons for taking the substance.

Lemon juice, with carbonate of potash, was a common drink used at the time to try to stop severe vomiting. This was simply a lemon-based drink. If he really had taken salts of lemon, that was a different matter, because this is an acid, potassium oxalate, and has no citric acid in it. It is a strong and poisonous acid used as a bleach, so in effect, he was thought to have taken

The Ring o' Bells *where Mr Mann enjoyed more than a tipple.* Laura Carter

bleach. It may be that Mann was terribly sickly and had taken some of the stuff to help, if he had taken a drink with citric acid; salts of lemon would indeed indicate a suicide attempt. Often, it was taken for stomach problems, as so many substances were then. It is worth recalling that this was an era when beershops were open in the morning and Mann was in a desperate condition in the early afternoon. It was also the time when countless popular remedies were for sale in the popular press for all kinds of real and perhaps imagined ailments, such as Hayman's Balsam for chests and 'Whelpton's Purifying Pills' for 'head-aches, bile and indigestion'.

However, the record spoke for itself: here was a man who had tried to take his own life before, and with a variety of drinks and foodstuffs. He may well have had what we would now call an eating disorder, or simply a need to try anything to counteract the effects of alcohol.

Whatever the reason, he found himself in court at the Bradford City Sessions on 14 January 1914; as the offence of attempted suicide was seen as a felony (called *felonia de se* – a felony against the self) he was sentenced to six months in prison with hard labour. The case may never have risen beyond the obscurity of so many similar cases had it not been for the debate at the appeal court on 9 February that year. Here was Mr Mann, having already been doing hard labour for several weeks, with his lawyers arguing that his offence was not a felony, and so he should not be labouring, but merely sewing mail bags in a prison workshop.

His lawyer, Mr Mockett, argued that the offence was a misdemeanour, the difference being that a felony meant that an offender's goods and chattels would be lost. If it were a misdemeanour, then Mann should have simply been given a straight gaol term.

The whole focus of the appeal was on the taking of the salts of lemon, and Mr Mann could not remember buying or taking them. He kept insisting that 'it never entered his head' to take his own life. This would have been hard to accept, given his habit of doing so and failing to succeed. The debate ended with the judge asserting that a felony had indeed been committed, but it reads as though his reading was based on the offender's past actions, rather than on what he did on this particular occasion.

Yet reason and humanity prevailed. Although, by the Hard Labour Act of 1833 his crime was a felony, and by the 1870 Fortfeiture Act the doubt was sorted out, after a rise in the number of wealthy young men with military connections taking their own lives, the Lord Chief Justice decided that the sentence should be custody only, with no hard labour: 'We think that restraint and discipline cannot injure the appellant ....'

Mann must have preferred that to breaking rocks with a sledgehammer; but equally, that situation may have presented him with other methods of *felo de se*.

CHAPTER 43

Last Words on the Blum Case 1866 (Unsolved)

... *an appointment with death.*

When I first approached this mystifying subject, and wrote about it in *Unsolved Yorkshire Murders* (2004), I had the details from Marie Campbell's account in her *Curious Tales of Old West Yorkshire* (1999). This is the story of Israel Blum and his journey from Bradford to the Wirral, where he appears to have had an appointment with death. The most detailed first account was back at the time of the disappearance in 1866, and printed in the *Keighley News*.

Blum was Second Master at Bradford High School and was said to live a regular, disciplined life, being a reliable and morally upright member of the school community. On the day he travelled out of town, never to be seen again alive by anyone who knew him, he had taught in the morning as usual, and then talked with another member of staff. We know that he bought a copy of Dickens's *David Copperfield* at Byles' bookshop and then went to the Midland Station.

On that occasion, he told lies to his colleague Anderson: he

Frontispiece to David Copperfield *showing a key scene in Blum's story, 1850 edition.* Author's collection

said he was planning to so some scientific work at home, whereas he was really dashing to catch a train. There has to be a reason for both the urgency and the need to evade telling not only the truth of his plans, but also to avoid mentioning his catching any train out of the city. So begins the first set of questions in this mystery.

The next questions concern the reasons why a man of this kind, with that social position, might leave for another city quite a long way from his home, with no clothes and no suitcase? That suggests a certain foreboding – that he knew this was his last journey in life. Yet there is an *unless*. Unless he was meeting someone with whom he was to have a business or personal encounter, settle something important, and then return to Bradford without delay. Such a meeting would have to be very urgent, and his haste suggests that.

Blum was not seen alive again; his body was found at Hoylake, close to the Mersey estuary. What calls for our attention now is the account of what Blum's body was like when found. A doctor and a constable had made statements and the newspaper report was that he was on a rock more or less in the foetal position. 'The face was calm, as if in sleep.' Now come the two intriguing details, and most thinking leads to a connection between them: first, that his throat was cut, with two slashes being made, and second, that his copy of *David Copperfield* was found that evening by a man at Redstones.

The inquest decided on a verdict of suicide, but some medical opinion disagreed, notably that of Dr Dodd from Hoylake, who suspected foul play. When eventually friends and colleagues travelled to Liverpool to confirm the identity of the dead man, they also insisted that suicide was an impossible cause of death. He had possibly been robbed, because he left

The Midland Hotel, *where Blum had a drink before leaving the city.*
The author

Illustration of the wreck from the 1850 edition of David Copperfield. Author's collection

home with a lot of cash (£16) and the body had only a few shillings on it. His watch and gold Albert chain were also missing.

When it is realised that Blum was engaged to a young woman who was living in London, there is an invitation to indulge in some Holmesian thinking, particularly when this letter written to her by Blum is studied (written in April, a few weeks before he left Bradford):

> *I had a strange letter from Leeds from a stranger who is staying here on business. He comes from Hamburg and wishes to see me. As it is impossible for me to go to Leeds until Saturday I must Consider meanwhile what to do. A strange thing is it not?*

This letter was taken to Merseyside on Blum's person.

The final part of the enigma is that Blum had a brother, and this man was hard up. Blum had met him once in Bradford, and had given him money. The brother had been staying in Hamburg but his aim was to emigrate eventually to Australia.

Enquiries found witnesses around Hoylake, including a woman who had seen Blum alive at around eight standing on the beach near what was an hotel at that time. But nothing came of this, and a request was made for a new enquiry. This was not held, but the Chester coroner spoke personally to staff in Bradford regarding the murder or suicide question. If it were murder following a theft, why were there still valuables on the body? More intriguing, why was his body drenched when there had been no high tide?

Marie Campbell tried to follow up records of the case, and to trace any further investigations. It appears that nothing came of this. She rightly points out interesting

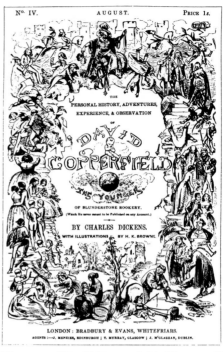

The cover of David Copperfield. *Blum would have read this in instalments. 1850 edition.* Author's collection

parallels between *David Copperfield* and the situation of Israel Blum: that his life and the plot have these things in common: a schoolmaster, and old school friend who dies in a storm at sea, a rich widow, and a close friend who goes to Australia. This puzzling parallel is probably the heart of the problem and we could speculate from this. It has to be said that shipwrecks and murder were also prominent in other very popular tales at exactly this time. Hannah Maria Jones's Penny Dreadful story, *The Shipwrecked Stranger* may also be relevant here. This was published in 1848, and includes the melodramatic narrative of a murderer and his being washed up after a shipwreck. But consider the possibilities of the story if it were to be a meeting with the mysterious man from Hamburg, about business, that went wrong; the 'business' may well have been related to debt – debts incurred by Blum's brother. The shipping links between

Liverpool and Hamburg were strong then, as now. The man who wrote from Leeds was German, and so was Blum; Blum's brother had lived in Hamburg. Those two simple facts invite some thinking based on links that are more than coincidence. We know that Blum's brother was short of money and was desperate to go to Australia to start a new life.

This opens up two possible scenarios: first, that the man who arranged a discreet meeting with Blum had mentioned the situation of the brother, and was pressurising Blum, because we know that Blum's brother had disappeared from Liverpool a few months before. He had something to run away from.

Blum, however, took only £16 with him, which suggests a plan to finance a few nights in a hotel (*The Royal Hotel* was near the beach where he was seen); it does not suggest that he was about to settle his tearaway brother's debts. Blum was a schoolmaster and about to be married; he would be comfortably off but not rich, and he would need his cash now that he would be supporting a wife.

The second possibility is that the death was indeed related to a bizarre fantasy related to the reading of *David Copperfield*. With this in mind, it helps to recall similar pacts which have involved a more than healthy imaginative involvement in works of art, in writing or painting that somehow becomes integral to the private imaginative life of two or more people. Given that Dickens's story is partly about betrayal and a friendship that ends in disillusionment, and does so with a massive imagery of the wild sea as a backdrop, it is possible this may be material here. This can only be reflected on by turning to that page that was turned down when the book was found: page 101.

It is tempting to follow the line of thought connected to what was very much in vogue in the literature and culture of the 1850s: male friendship. Literary historians such as Carolyn Oulton have studied this and noted that at that time, 'romantic friendship, although largely inaccessible to modern ideals, enjoyed a high . . . cultural status in the nineteenth century. The form of friendship depended on both strong feelings and . . . startling rhetorical expression.' In other words, male friends could and did make grand, passionate and sometimes fantastical gestures regarding the closeness of the friendship. Oulton points out that David Copperfield has this kind of relationship with the 'bounder', Steerforth.

Even more interesting, as Oulton notes, in the novel, Steerforth 'appropriates David's personal belongings and changes his name.' This is temptingly a possibility to explain the tryst kept by Blum. Can this reading of the crime make sense? Can Blum's reading of the novel help to relate this male friendship to the sad case of Israel Blum? We need to know about that page.

First, what edition had Mr Blum bought and taken on the train journey with him? The two possibilities are the 1858 cheap edition and the 1859 library edition. The cheap edition was in one volume, so he had to have bought the library edition which was published by Chapman and Hall. Volume two came out in April 1859 at a cost of six shillings: an expensive purchase. In fact, it would hardly be a book to buy specifically for a train journey, so did Israel Blum have a particular reason for having that specific book, and therefore was page 101 important and linked to a meeting in Hoylake, and indeed to his violent death? That page is in a chapter called 'Enthusiasm' and the material there concerns the planned leaving of the lovable wastrel, Wilkins Micawber, to take up a new life as a clerk to Uriah Heep in Canterbury. Like Blum, David first learns of this when he receives a letter, and the letter is an invitation to a celebratory gathering at Micawber's place, and both David and his friend Traddles set off for the dinner. But the other part of the chapter, covering page 101, concerns a discussion of the return from India of Jack Maldon. Both elements of the plot lead us nowhere in particular: a departure of an eccentric and an arrival of an old school companion.

Yet the meeting at the centre of this section is that of a tutor and a former pupil, and it is about money. Teacher and student discuss some planned work on the dictionary – the tutor's lifelong project – and then Maldon and the tutor have an odd conversation when Maldon is asked if there is any news. He replies that the people in the North are always discontented, and then he says:

> *There's a long statement in the papers, sir, about a murder. . . .*
> *But somebody is always being murdered and I didn't read it.*

In trying to work up a theory about the strange death of the Bradford teacher, we are left with several possibilities. If Blum had a fatal appointment, a bizarre sort of pact perhaps, with his penniless brother or indeed with another reader of the Dickens novel, then the evidence for that is inconclusive. He may have been attacked, but the motive is unlikely to have been for the money he was carrying. The final possibility is that he had a cheque or banker's draft with him, in addition to the eight pounds we know about, maybe to settle a debt.

The Hamburg connection is intriguing also, with the Liverpool–Hamburg sailing connections so obviously a link. But in the end, the Blum affair is shrouded in mystery. Any new lines of thought will be welcome from readers of this book. The official documentation is as mysterious as the facts of the last journey the unfortunate teacher took on that trip westwards. As Marie Campbell has noted, there was a photograph taken of Blum's corpse and a print was given to the Home Office. But there is no trace of this anywhere. There is no photograph of the victim in The National Archives, and as Marie says, 'a professional researcher has also been unsuccessful in locating information about Mr Israel James Blum in national repositories.'

When all the obvious lines of thought have been considered to be untenable, perhaps we are left with the uncanny link with the Dickens novel after all: death pact or unseemly killing, brother on brother, all for the cost of a ship abroad, away from the debtors in pursuit. Blum's brother was his own imagined Steerforth, perhaps, and the teacher gave his life as well as his money for the dark alter ego he met that day near Hoylake.

Sources and Bibliography

Books and periodicals

Anderson, O, *Suicide in Victorian and Edwardian Britain*, Oxford University Press, 1987.

Baines's Yorkshire Directory 1822, The author, London, 1822.

Barber, B J, *Guide to the Quarter sessions of the West Riding of Yorkshire*, West Yorkshire Archive Consultation Council, 1984.

Bloom, C, *Violent London*, Pan Books, 2003.

Briggs, A, *Victorian Cities*, Penguin, 1968.

Burnley, J, *West Riding Sketches*, Hodder and Stoughton, 1875.

Burnley, J, *The Romance of Modern Industry*, W H Allen, 1889.

Campbell, M, *Curious Tales of Old West Yorkshire*, Sigma, 1999.

Canter, D, *Mapping Murder*, Virgin, 2003.

Cawley, A C (Ed.), *A Yorkshire Tragedy*, Manchester University Press, 1986.

Cornwell, P, *Portrait of a Killer: Jack the Ripper case closed*, Time Warner, 2002.

Cross, R, *The Yorkshire Ripper*, Harper Collins, 1995.

Dewhirst, I, *Gleanings from Victorian Yorkshire*, Ridings Publishing, 1972.

Dickens, C, *David Copperfield*, Oxford University Press, 1999.

Dictionary of Law, Third Edition, Oxford University Press, 1994.

Eddleston, J J, *The Encyclopaedia of Executions*, John Blake, 2002.

Emsley, C, *Crime and Society in England 1750–1900*, Pearson, 1996.

Evans, S P, *Executioner: The Chronicles of James Berry, Victorian Hangman*, Sutton, 2004.

Forshaw, C (Ed.), *Yorkshire Notes and Queries*.

Foster, R F, *Paddy and Mr Punch*, Allen Lane, 1993.

Grey, D (Ed. S J Pimm), *The Facts behind the Guard House Murder 1864, Keighley*, Whins Wood Publishing House, Keighley, 1996.

Harrison, J F C, *Early Victorian Britain*, Fontana, 1988.

Hovell, M, *The Chartist Movement*, Manchester University Press, 1918.

Jennings, P, *Bradford Pubs*, Tempus, 2004.

Jones, S, *Yorkshire, The Sinister Side Book 1 1850–80*, Wicked Books, 2004.

Journal of the Police History Society, No. 19, 2004.

Kelly, A, *The Trial of Feargus O'Connor*, author, 1848.

Kilday, A-M and Watson, K, 'Child Murder in Georgian England', in *History Today*, Vol. 55, January, 2001 pp. 40–46.

Household Narrative, Chapman and Hall, 1850.

Lane, B, *The Encyclopaedia of Forensic Science*, Headline, 1992.

Langan, P, *Valleys of Death*, Breedon Books, 2001.

Newman, P R, *The Royal Castle of York*, York Castle Museum, 2004.

Owens, A and Ellis, C, *Killer Catchers*, John Blake, 2004.

Priestley, J B, *English Journey*, Heinemann, 1994.

Punch: Mr Punch In Wig and Gown: The Lighter Side of Bench and Bar, Educational Book Co, 1890.

Rede, T L, *York Castle*, Saunders, 1829.

Royle, E, *Chartism*, Longman, 1986.

Robertson Scott, J W, *The Day Before Yesterday*, Methuen, 1951.

Sharpe, J, *Dick Turpin*, Profile Books, 2004.

Stallion, M and Wall, D S, *The British Police: Police Forces and Chief Officers 1829–2000*, Police History Society, 1999.

Styles, J, 'An Eighteenth-Century Magistrate as Detective: Samuel Lister of Little Horton', *The Bradford Antiquary*, Vol. 10, pp. 98-117, 1982.

Thompson, E P, *The Making of the English Working Class*, Penguin, 1991.

Thompson, D, *The Early Chartists*, Macmillan, 1971.

Tibballs, G, *The Murder Guide to Great Britain*, Boxtree, 1993.

Turner, E S, *Roads to Ruin: the Shocking History of Social Reform*, Macmillan, 1974.

White, R J, *Waterloo to Peterloo*, Peregrine, 1968.

Wilson, C and Seaman, D, *The Serial Killers*, Virgin Publishing, 2000.

Wilson, C and Wilson, D, *World Famous Unsolved Crimes*, Constable and Robinson, 2004.

Wright, D G, *The Chartist Risings in Bradford*, Bradford Libraries and Information Service, 1987.

Newspaper archives

Bradford Telegraph and Argus
The Leeds Mercury
The Northern Star
The Yorkshire Post

Non-Book Sources

The Ultimate Price: The unlawful killing of British Police Officers (in two parts), by Paul R L Williams (www.murderfiles.com).
Real Life Crimes, Eaglemoss, 2003.

Index

(1) People

(2) Places